PARTING
THE
WATERS

PARTING
THE
WATERS

*How Vision and Faith
Make Good Business*

JAMES VINCENT

MOODY PRESS
CHICAGO

ISBN: 0-8024-5934-X

3 5 7 9 10 8 6 4 2

Printed in the United States of America

To Jonathan and Daniel,
my sons who laugh and splash
upon the waters;
and to Lori, my wife,
who loves the Master
who calmed the sea

Contents

Acknowledgments

*F*or almost seventy-five years, one recreational boat company has parted the waters, building quality ski boats and remaining true to the desire of its founder to honor God. Over several months, many individuals guided the author to the heart of this company and its owners, the Meloon family. I wish to acknowledge all who have helped me to report the story of Correct Craft.

David and Dorothy Enlow first told the story of the vision and faith of the company in *Saved from Bankruptcy.* Years later, Robert Flood updated the story of the miraculous repayment of all their creditors and the company's unwavering principles in *On the Waters of the World.* Now *Parting the Waters* looks at the Meloons' continuing adherence to business ethics and Christian values. My thanks to the Enlows and Flood for their initial reporting; portions of both accounts are included in this book.

Terri Garner, manager of ski shows at Sea World of Florida, helped me tell the story of how Correct Craft's boats are helping her skiers perform at their best at the Orlando theme park. Andy Hansen, a former ski show director at Sea World, provided valuable perspective on the Christian faith among show skiers, and his own testimony reveals a man who wants to know God better. You will find Terri and Andy's stories in chapter 12.

My thanks to Van Thurston and Charles Brock, two caring men who continue to help the Meloons to declare the truths of God's good plans when we are in deepest waters. Van explained the hopes and heart of Turnaround Ministries. Charles prepared and rushed to me valuable recordings of a recent Turnaround Weekend just days before this manuscript was due. Charles and his wife, Joyce, were servants during my weekend visit to a Turnaround Weekend in Arrowhead Springs in San Bernardino, California. They have learned that when it comes to trusting God, "It is always too soon to quit."

Many employees and managers at Correct Craft helped in telling the story of this company. My special thanks to three of them: Larry Meddock, Angela Pilkington, and Ruth Ward. Larry taught me to better understand inboard boats, water-ski competition, and the principles of this boatbuilding company. He also spent much time discussing his personal journey to faith. Angela, the company's office manager, and Ruth, secretary to the senior Meloons, helped me track down documents and arrange interviews during my two visits to company headquarters in Orlando.

My special gratitude to the Meloon family, who gave many hours to interviews. W. N. Meloon, president of Correct Craft, demonstrated a candor and passion to honor God that's refreshing. Ralph Meloon, chairman of the board, met me in Florida, Illinois, and California to answer my questions and to offer help at any time. By his words and actions, he demonstrates that we "can never give to the Lord. We only return what He has given us." And Walter O. Meloon, treasurer of the board, provided much insight into the company. His humility and compassion continue to touch everyone he meets.

Finally, I am deeply grateful to my wife, Lori, who in gentle, thoughtful ways helped me to find time in the evenings and weekends to sort through notes and papers to prepare this book. She was my balance wheel, reminding me of her love and my duties to our boys. Thanks for being there, my dear Lori.

Chapter 1
Storm Boats to the Rescue

*A*merica was still at war in December 1944. Families
with servicemen overseas found the Christmas season
tinged with uncertainty and fear. They prayed. They
hoped. They listened to the radio as soldiers and sailors fought
World War II in Europe and the Pacific. And just before the holiday, they found mixed comfort in the results of a battle with an
unusual name. The Battle of the Bulge began days before Christmas, as Adolf Hitler's troops staged a massive counterattack
against advancing Allied forces. The Nazi war machine inflicted
major damage, yet Hitler's army also suffered heavy losses—
losses he could not afford. Though many Americans were
unaware, the Third Reich had begun to crumble.

Gen. Dwight D. Eisenhower and his forces moved rapidly,
pushing steadily through France, Belgium, and across the borders into Germany, toward Berlin itself. Victory seemed near,
yet one major obstacle still stood before them, the Rhine River.
Since the time of Napoleon, this swift, muddy river had held
Germany's enemies at bay. How would the Allies cross the
Rhine?

The very success of the Allied drive created another problem. Because Eisenhower was weeks ahead of schedule, his
armies were approaching the banks of the Rhine without enough

boats to make a safe crossing for troops or equipment. The general pondered his strategy. He knew he would face a crucial loss of time and men unless he could cross the river quickly. He earmarked March 10 as the best date for the operation.

His cable to Washington was an SOS, appealing for 700 storm boats by early March. The compact, seventeen-foot vessels, with their spoon-shaped bows, were tailor-made for such maneuvers. The highly expendable boats could skid up onto beaches at full throttle.

In Florida, the Correct Craft company was one of several suppliers that had been building boats for the military. In fact, the company had already signed a contract to supply twenty assault boats a month when government officials placed an emergency call from Washington on February 9. But Correct Craft had shut down that day in honor of a friend's funeral being held in a nearby church. W. C. Meloon, founder of the company, was at the service with his three sons—Walt (also known as W. O.), Ralph, and Harold—all of whom worked with him. When they returned to the plant, the watchman handed W. C. a message: Army engineers had been trying to reach him all afternoon, calling from a district office in Jacksonville, a division office in Atlanta, and the chief's office in Washington, D.C.

When W. C. returned the call, the chief engineer explained Eisenhower's situation. "Look," he said, "here's some classified information so you can understand how important this is: General Eisenhower has set March 10 as the day to cross the Rhine River. We must get as many boats there as possible or our troops will run out of food and all supplies by staying [penned up] there.

"If possible, we need 700 boats. How many storm boats can you build by February 28 with a triple-A preference rating and all the cooperation possible from U. S. engineers?"

W. C. answered immediately, "Well, the family will talk and pray tonight, and tomorrow we'll tell you what we will do." Then he and his sons conferred and prayed.

THREE HUNDRED BOATS IN ONE MONTH

The next morning, W. C. called the army man. "If God is in it," he said, "we believe it's possible to build 300 boats."

"We didn't know how to build 300 when we said that," W. O. now admits, "but God showed us how."

The firm's normal February schedule called for building forty-eight boats. Retooling and gearing up for six times that amount was an impossible task, friends assured them. They would need more workers, and many male laborers were unavailable, serving in the military. Yet the Meloons had confidence in God's ability to do the impossible as they did their part.

The next day, the plant geared up for the increased production. The Meloon family and their employees worked until midnight building jigs—open frames for holding work and guiding machine tools to the work. They made preliminary plans to start production. After stopping to rest on Sunday, they resumed work at 1:00 A.M. Monday. That day, they increased their crew from 60 employees to 320. The company quickly hired scores of women to replace all the male boatbuilders who were in the armed forces.

As W. O. recalls, many of the new boatbuilders were women "who had husbands and brothers overseas. Those women joined the war right then. They were ready to work, and they produced like you couldn't believe."

Like the other private contractors making storm boats, Correct Craft faced multiple problems: scarcity of materials, uncertain transportation, new and inexperienced help, and shortage of time. The Army Corps of Engineers sent help as had been promised, including a plant engineer and a staff of inspectors.

Still, only fifteen days remained to complete 300 boats.

The Corps of Engineers helped all the boatbuilders to meet the rush deadline. One materials expediter came to Orlando, home of Correct Craft, to help locate supplies and specialty tools for the task. The key component was plywood, not in large supply during wartime. The Corps helped the boatbuilders secure sheets of it from Pacific Northwest lumber mills and then had the wood flown cross-country to the eastern boat shops. It was winter, of course, and in some cases truck drivers with vital supplies crawled over mountainous roads while storms raged so fiercely that no other vehicles had ventured out. All the trucks were able to deliver without a single accident. It was an answer to prayer.

SUNDAY: A DAY OF REST

Government expediters offered many good suggestions. But one requirement was unacceptable to the management of Correct Craft. An army colonel asked the company to keep its doors open seven days a week to meet the deadline. The Meloons responded with a polite but firm no.

"We intend to do the job to the glory of God," W. C. said. "It's not His plan to work seven days a week."

The colonel argued that the company needed the three extra days to accomplish the task. The Meloons stood their ground, quoting two scriptures: "Remember the sabbath day, to keep it holy"; "Them that honour me I will honour" (Exodus 20:8; 1 Samuel 2:30, KJV). W. C. had become convicted years before of the importance of honoring God by observing a weekly day of rest.

The Meloons did not give in, even though they knew a possible legal battle with the government might wipe them out. They pressed the discussion. "Look," W. C. told the official, "we're working our people sometimes eighteen hours a day on one shift. They can't take it anymore. In fact, God built this world in six days and rested on the seventh. That's what we're going to do, and we're going to trust Him for the results."

The Corps of Engineers was surprised by the company's response. All the other boat makers operated on Sundays, but Correct Craft made sure its people rested on Sundays so they could go to church and have one day of special worship. And, as W. O. told the Corps, it made good business sense, too, because effective workers are rested workers. Everyone needs a time for physical and spiritual renewal.

W. O. also explained, "Listen, if we win this war, it will be because God wants us to win. It won't be solely because of the effort you make or we make or anyone else makes. If God wants us to win this war, we'll win it. But if He doesn't, we'll lose it!"

"If you insist," W. C. finally said, "you can have the contract back. This job is impossible for man to do alone."

The Corps listened and finally agreed. It dropped the requirement and waited to see if the company would finish the job on time.

Similar conflicts arose at Correct Craft's other plant in Titusville, Florida. There the Meloons built boats for the navy, including plane-rearming boats, navy whaleboats, and plane-personnel boats. Government policy restricted the awarding of contracts when builders serviced more than one branch of the military at a time. Providentially, the Meloons believe, contracts came from the army and navy on the same day and remained in effect with government approval.

A navy inspector in Titusville told the firm it could not take time out for weekly chapel services. The boatbuilders again responded firmly: "If we can't serve the Lord and the U.S. Navy at the same time, we just won't serve the navy."

The navy commander in Jacksonville finally realized the unyielding stand of the family and overruled his subordinate. "You won't have any further problem with the inspector on this," he assured them.

On Monday, February 12, the company had built its first storm boat. What seemed like an agonizingly slow process began to improve. Workers built three boats on Tuesday and seven on Wednesday. Some of the employees shook their heads in disbelief when the Meloons called a halt for the midweek chapel service in the plant. With three of the fifteen workdays gone, only eleven boats had been built.

That night, the entire Meloon family met together for prayer. They prayed more desperately than ever before, asking God to show them how to complete the job.

W. O., the oldest son, awakened the next morning with an idea that would speed production. A new machine and a change on the jig were the answer. He made the change, and Ralph located a man who could build the new machine. He needed the rest of the week to complete the work. Production accelerated with the change on the jig.

On Thursday, February 15, less than two weeks from their deadline, the workers built 13 boats. On Friday, they built 17; on Saturday, 21. Still, with six of the fifteen workdays gone, only 62 of the 300 boats had been built.

The work crew rested again on Sunday, then resumed production early Monday morning, February 19. Refreshed by the day of rest and with the new machine in action, they rapidly moved ahead.

What followed, journalist Jim Harmon wrote years later in *Powerboat* magazine, "was comparable to cramming two hours of music onto a 30-minute cassette."[1] Production was accelerating, and two days later an army colonel flew down from Atlanta and found boats stacked all over the plant and spilling into the street in front. With state and village approval, Orange Avenue had been blocked off, and boats were being stored in the streets. Later that year, *National Geographic* published a photo of that memorable scene—a street filled with boats and a sign in the foreground stating the obvious: "Road Closed" and, in smaller letters, "Detour."[2]

The plant hummed with activity. By now the 320 men and women workers were building up to 42 boats a day. A local minister presided at the midweek chapel service. He invited the colonel to say a few words to the employees. Standing atop a cutting bench in the middle of the blocked-off Florida highway, the officer looked down into the faces of the workers.

"Men and women," he said, "you have done a remarkable job, and I want to compliment you. I have just visited three other plants in the north where they are working on this same job, and all of them together are not doing what you are doing."

Encouraged by those remarks and a conviction that God

was working, the Meloons and their colaborers returned to their task with new zeal.

During the second six-day workweek, the inspired and efficient crew built 240 more boats. Amazingly, no rain fell to slow production, even though February typically is the wettest month of the year in Orlando. At noon on Saturday, February 24, a jubilant crowd of boatbuilders stood on the sidetrack and saw an express train haul away the 306th boat. The army engineer in charge of the special project said, "There goes our quota four days ahead of schedule. Someone other than man did this job. If it had rained only one day, we couldn't have accomplished it."

ONE HUNDRED MORE BOATS

A day earlier, the plant had received a special request from the chief of the Corps of Engineers. Would Correct Craft build another 100 boats? The other three contractors, he said, had fallen short of their quotas.

The Meloons said yes. With the accelerated operation now in full swing, the workers built another 100 boats in the final four days of February. In all, they delivered 406 storm boats. The final 100 boats were sent to New York in fruit trucks, the best ground transportation available at the time, and then flown to Europe.

Made of inexpensive, flexible, birch plywood, the boats would slide right onto shore, where ten soldiers could charge up the beach and into the hills beyond. The troops would not look back as the outboard engines kept running. The boats were completely disposable, with only one goal: to storm the beach and discharge their passengers.

"When the storm boats produced by the other builders arrived at the Rhine," W. O. says, "the army couldn't use them. The specs were wrong, and the engines wouldn't fit. Ours were the only ones built right."

W. O. doesn't believe the other companies built their boats incorrectly because they had the wrong specifications. "They

had received the same specifications we had," he says. "For
some reason, they did not follow the specs; we did, the engines
fit on them, and the boats crossed the river successfully." He
speculates that replacement workers at the other companies
were either not well trained or not well rested, as they had been
given no Sundays off.

The only special preparation the Correct Craft replacement workers had received before they began building the
assault boats was to view one already made. Management had
bought one from another boatbuilder assigned to the project.
They hoisted the craft above a blueprint. It was a valuable
model, according to W. O.: "Our workers could see it over the
blueprint and visualize how to loft [curve] the boat and compare it to their patterns."

Plant workers prayed for the success of the Rhine crossing with extra fervor. The crossing went smoothly. The assault
boats, all manufactured by Correct Craft, gave the soldiers several crossing points along the river. The advantage to that
approach was that if Hitler's troops were watching the river, the
Americans were safer being spread out rather than following
one another across a bridge. More than four thousand soldiers
crossed in the boats that day.

The Allies got a "bonus" crossing as well. Somehow the
Nazis failed to blow up a railroad bridge at Remagen on the
Rhine before the Allies arrived. Hitler was furious. Two days
later, he executed the three men whom he held responsible for
what may have been the greatest blunder of the war. As the
Remagen bridge stayed up, the Americans had continued
access across the Rhine after the boat crossing, and vital supplies flowed freely. But the boat crossing had been crucial,
creating a beachhead that would allow the Allies to move ever
closer to Berlin. By May 8, 1945, the war in Europe was officially over.

Later that month, the United States military remembered
the number and quality of the assault boats produced by Correct Craft and called it a miracle. On May 23, 1945, the U. S.

government, in a special ceremony at the Orlando plant, awarded the company the army and navy "E" award. And in Washington, D. C., the government listed the boatbuilding achievement on its records as "the miracle production."

Visitors from all parts of the United States for many weeks thereafter came to see the place where a company could build 400 boats in fifteen working days—without infringing on the Lord's Day.

On March 2, just days after Correct Craft had shipped the final boats, the colonel who had insisted the company work seven days a week returned to the plant. He now stood in front of the shop, tears glistening on his cheeks.

"You folks certainly have faith in the Lord," he said. "I want to congratulate you." He then shook hands with W. C. and his three sons.

The Meloon family attributed all honor to the God who had led and strengthened them. W. O. smiles as he recalls the outcome: "It's called a miracle in boatbuilding. To us, it was simply an indication that the Lord honors the obedience of His children."

TO THE GLORY OF GOD

As remarkable as the outstanding and on-time production of those 406 storm boats was, it's only one episode in the exciting story of a company that from its beginning in 1925 was dedicated to the glory of God. Today, the company is better known for its long and close association with one of America's most popular and fastest-growing sports.

Ironically, this sport that depends on warm weather got its start in Minnesota.

Notes

1. Jim Harmon, "The Meloons: Three Parts Know-How, Three Parts Faith," *Power-boat,* August 1982, 46.
2. "Winning the War in Supply," *National Geographic,* December 1945, 734.

Chapter 2

Atop the Waters

*B*rad Henry, a seven-year-old with brown hair and slight build, knew it was time to learn to water-ski on Lake Metigoshe in North Dakota. His parents, both skiers themselves, had told him so. Once his skis were fixed properly to his small feet, Brad waited in the cool water.

Four times, as his dad added throttle to the ski boat's engine, Brad rose to the surface, only to fall either forward or backward, taking turns splashing his face and bumping his backside. On the fifth try, he finally got partly up before falling again.

Some would-be skiers might give up at that point, but Brad had seen his parents and friends ski enough to know that he could do it. He realized he had to keep his skis under control and "beneath my body."

So for a sixth time he came up from the water. But now he held on and was standing—moving forward. Success!

"Once I was out of the water, a lot of the drag was gone, and it was a lot easier," Brad said. "It felt almost freeing. Standing on those skis, I knew I had accomplished something."

Today Brad is a show skier at Sea World of Florida, performing up to five times each day during the summer months. At age thirty-two he rarely falls, and he still enjoys that feeling of freedom, racing along on top of the waters.

Not many water-skiers become show professionals, of course. Most ski just for the fun of it, like twelve-year-old Kelsey Dokkestul and her two brothers, Joel and Josh. They started skiing lessons recently after the whole family had moved to Clermont, Florida (about thirty miles from Orlando). The children lived within a block of Buck Lake, and they watched their friends ski the first summer.

After lessons on land and in the water using an extended ski pylon, Kelsey was ready for her third lesson; she would have a deep-water start with the towrope attached to a regular ski pylon. Her instructor gave her some final reminders. "Keep your arms straight and your knees bent. And keep your rope between the skis."

A light drizzle fell on this unusually cool September day in central Florida as the boat started moving. Kelsey quickly came atop the waters. Almost as quickly she fell, twice. "I tried to pull myself up," Kelsey explained. On her third try, she got up and moving. For forty-five wonderful seconds, she skimmed across the lake.

"I felt good coming up, and I felt pretty good about myself," Kelsey says.

WIND, WATER, AND FUN

Ten-year-old Joel got up the first time, and he remembers the wind and the wet. "I felt lots of wind and the water in my face," he says. "Some was from the skis, but some was the drizzle from the rain. I was blinking my eyes, but it was fun." And older brother Josh, age fifteen, found skiing just as fun.

The Dokkestul children and Brad Henry are among more than 13 million Americans who love to ride across the country's lakes and rivers on fiberglass water skis.[1] Atop the waters, they enjoy those feelings of freedom and fun—of wind in the hair, speed on their feet, and, at times, the light bump of crossing the boat's wake as they skim along.

Most skiers don't think much about the sport's origins or the developments along the way that make waterskiing today safe and relatively easy to learn. (Unlike Brad, who had no lessons, those who take classes are usually up by their second attempt.) Many innovators and visionaries helped make water-skiing the popular sport it is, but among the pioneers, two names stand out: Ralph Samuelson and the boatbuilding company, Correct Craft. The name Correct Craft, with its line of Ski Nautique boats preferred by tournament skiers, is probably the better known of the two. Samuelson deserves equal credit, however, for he was the first to put skis on his feet and skim atop the waters. Later Correct Craft would market the skis commercially and help get the sport off the ground.

ATOP THE WATERS IN MINNESOTA

The sport of waterskiing got its start in 1922, when Ralph Samuelson first attached a couple of barrel staves to his feet and skimmed across Lake Pepin, Minnesota, about sixty miles south of Minneapolis. For the next thirty years, however, others were getting the credit. Some thought skiing began in Seattle in 1928, when Don Ibsen rode his own pair of homemade skis; others said the sport began the same year in Miami Beach, where Dick and Malcomb Pope drew crowds with their own water-ski exhibitions just years before Dick's ski shows at Cypress Gardens would popularize the sport.[2] Not even the American Water Ski Association knew for certain where the fast-growing sport had originated.

Finally, Ralph "Sammy" Samuelson spoke up in 1963. He had never patented his skis, but he had compelling evidence. His story was told in the *Orlando Tribune,* from which this account is adapted.[3]

A tall, rangy Swede who hadn't been in church since he was nine, Ralph had been forced to grow up quickly, helping to support a family of five kids and an alcoholic father. Among his jobs were helping in the local nursery, pulling weeds, and being a fisherman and a clammer. He owned his own boat at one time, and he knew and loved Lake Pepin. Yet since age ten, one

idea kept coming back to him: *Every winter, my brothers and
I ski on snow. Why can't we ski on water in the summer?*

And every summer he tried it with different devices, primarily snow skis and barrel staves. He attached a towline to his
brother Ben's smelly clam boat. But when the line tightened,
Ralph sank every time.

One summer day, the young man tried a new design. He
bought two planks from a local lumberyard, each eight feet long
and nine inches wide. Back home, he stuck the tips into his
mother's copper wash kettle and boiled them for three hours.
Next, he fastened the two pieces in a vise and kept them under
stress for two days until they were permanently curved. Then he
nailed a piece of rubber matting and a leather foot strap to each.
Finally, he picked up the staves and an old clothesline with a
metal ring fastened to one end and headed again to deep water.

But again and again, down went Ralph.

Finally, on Sunday, July 2, 1922, as most people went to
church, Ralph was back on the water with his new design. He
was on the lake all morning, trying to skim atop the water. And
then it happened.

"I didn't deserve it," Samuelson recalled, "but God had
plans for me, so at 4:11 P.M., a voice told me to keep the tips of
my monstrous skis *out* of the water when I started. And there I
was, skimming on top of the waves like a water bug. Not that
anybody cared. But it was a great satisfaction to me. I had finally
proved to my friends that I was not a complete fool.

"But I didn't have the faintest idea what I had started."

Ralph turned nineteen the next day and began to improve
his technique. He gave skiing demonstrations on the lake but
never earned a penny with his new skill. All entrance fees collected at the Sunday water carnivals were used by the local
chamber of commerce to buy land for a modern marina. The
next summer, Ralph became the world's first water-ski jumper,
flying off an inclined diving platform. At first he nearly had his
arm yanked out, and his rump got tattooed with splinters, until
he greased the boards with lard from Huettle's meat market.

In 1925, Samuelson added another first when he skied eighty miles per hour behind Walter Bullock's reconstructed World War I flying boat.

He later performed with his giant skis in Detroit, near a cousin's place, and in southern Florida, where his father owned land. The crowds roared, and Ralph loved the cheers.

But one day as he helped construct a new dock, the supporting props gave way under a section of a wooden platform. A friend panicked, and single-handedly Ralph held up the platform section long enough for a fellow worker to scramble to safety. He saved the man's life but broke his back in the process —a compression fracture.

He was an invalid. His waterskiing was ended forever.

Ralph was bitter. Why had God, if there was a God, let this happen to him?

FROM SKIS TO TURKEYS

Back in Lake City, the two skis went up into the rafters of an old fish house. Eventually Ralph married, moved to a small farm, and decided to try raising turkeys. Much to the surprise of his friends, he succeeded. At one point he had the largest turkey farm in Minnesota. His modern hatcheries and feeders produced lots of healthy turkeys, and success breeded success. Ralph became rich; his fleet featured racing boats, an airplane, and a couple of Lincoln Continentals.

"Then God really fixed me," said Ralph. "He took me down twenty pegs. It began when I learned that my wife was unfaithful to me—had been for ten years. Everybody knew it but me."

The blow to Ralph's ego was almost fatal. He contemplated suicide.

"Then one night, out under His stars, while I was shouting to Him to help me or end my life, God spoke to me, laid His hand on me, and saved me. I became His," Ralph said. *How* it happened he didn't know. *Why* it happened Ralph did know.

He gave up his drinking, cursing, and smoking. And some

time after his divorce, he married a Christian woman, Hazel Thorpe, whom he met one Christmas morning in church. He knew "God wanted me to work for Him." For a time, though, Ralph refused.

The turkey business continued to prosper, and Ralph added farms and a beautiful dream house. Then another tragedy struck. In three successive years, plagues hit his beautiful flocks of bronze turkeys in spite of the efforts of the best experts: cholera, erysipelas, paratyphoid. His stock was devastated, and soon he had more debts than assets.

"This time God was really tired of my pride, I guess," Ralph believed. "He made me feel the way Job must have felt— at his worst."

Like Job, Ralph's faith was tested; and like Job, he clung to his God. "The only thing that kept me going was my faith. I felt, somehow, that eventually God was going to use me, although I didn't know how. Time after time, I nearly despaired." Now the once-star skier and former turkey farmer wanted to serve God, but he felt his position had been taken away. "I was nothing— dirt. It seems that in our country, people don't want to listen to nobodies, certainly not to a busted, retired turkey farmer. They said the faith I was yapping about was foolish."

But those oversized skis, now stashed in the rafters of his big barn, would show the inventor/farmer was no fool. The annual water carnival was coming up in Lake City, and the harbormaster wanted an eye-catching display for the largest display window in town. As a young man, Ben Simons had watched Ralph do his first stunt on water skis. Now, as harbormaster, he would track Samuelson down and find those big skis.

"WORLD'S FIRST WATER SKIS"

Simons located Ralph counting turkeys. After a brief conversation, they retrieved the skis, dusted them off, and put them on display. The homemade sign read: "World's First Water Skis."

Most residents read the sign and were skeptical. How could Ben get hold of the world's first pair of skis? After the carnival, he stored them in the attic of a store he owned. In 1963, he nailed them up as a wall decoration at the city's new bathhouse. Below them, he placed the same homemade sign.

Then Margaret Crimmins, a young sportswriter for the St. Paul *Pioneer-Press,* spent a vacation at Lake City, saw the old skis in the bathhouse, and wrote a feature about them. She actually tried on the vintage skis and loved them, concluding the piece that ran in the next Sunday's edition, "Your old skis are great. Where are you, Mr. Samuelson?"

Ralph saw it, and suddenly God's purpose became clear. He was to be anonymous no longer. Then perhaps people would listen to him as he witnessed for Christ.

"By becoming the world's first water-skier," said Ralph, "God was giving me a tool that I would eventually use in His service." First Ralph, the harbormaster, and the young sportswriter documented his claim to be the world's first water-skier. At the St. Paul Historical Society, they found old copies of now-defunct 1922 newspapers to prove, with pictures, that Ralph had actually water-skied that year. Next they wrote to the American Water Ski Association in Winter Haven, Florida, with corroborating evidence and statements by eyewitnesses.

Eventually, Ralph's challenge won. The other claimants, including a ski maker on the French Riviera, had to admit Ralph had done it first. He was officially proclaimed the father of waterskiing.

In 1972, Lake City celebrated its centennial and simultaneously the fiftieth anniversary of waterskiing. Ralph gained international publicity on radio, television, and in the printed press. A few years later, in September 1976, Lake City unveiled another monument in his honor, a huge, stylized wave, near the actual cove where he first came up out of the water.

In his acceptance speech, Ralph gave all credit to God: "Without Him, I would be nothing. He has brought me out of anonymity to let me spread the message that He is great."

Ralph Samuelson died in 1977, one year after giving that testimony. His skis now are exhibit 1 in the new Water Ski Hall

of Fame near Lakeland, Florida. And people will still remember
Ralph Samuelson in 2076, because in the time capsule that will
be opened at Valley Forge, Pennsylvania, at America's tricenten-
nial is a bronze replica of his first skis.

THE FIRST TOURNAMENT WATER SKIS

Samuelson's creation in the Minnesota north woods did
not receive notice right away because he didn't put his water skis
into commercial production. Down in Orlando, however, a
small but innovative boat company did, drawing attention to an
emerging sport. The skis made by the Florida Variety Boat Company, the predecessor of Correct Craft, were smaller yet stronger
than Samuelson's. They would propel Dick Pope's Miami Beach
skiers and later performers at Pope's Cypress Gardens.

Those small, wooden boards became the first show and
tournament skis ever made. The improved version used two
thin pieces of wood glued together, making the skis more
durable and less likely to split. The ski became popular especially for ski jumping, where it easily withstood impact jump
after jump. For a while, the Florida Variety Boat Company was
the sole builder of skis, according to Walt O. (W. O.) Meloon,
son of the founder.

"The two thin pieces of wood could do two things," W. O.
says. "They could hold shape as you bent and glued them. And
with the wood grains in slightly different directions, the skis
were stronger."

Meloon's ski was much thinner than Samuelson's pio-
neering version. "His ski was long and wide; it would plane
behind a small boat," W. O. explains. Meloon designed a ski
one-third the size of Samuelson's to skim behind the faster
inboard towboat. "Ours was similar to a snow ski, probably a
little wider and a little longer."

Correct Craft made its last pair of skis in 1950; today
water skis feature brilliant colors and fiberglass construction.
The company has continued to develop the sport, though, with
a list of innovations, including the first ski pylon and the first

tracking fin for inboard towboats. Its impact on waterskiing has been acknowledged. W. O. has been inducted into the Water Ski Hall of Fame. The Meloon family—W. O., Ralph, and W. O.'s son Walt N.—have received waterskiing's Award of Distinction. One industry watcher declared that W. O. and Ralph, Correct Craft's chairman of the board, "have done as much to promote organized water skiing as anyone in the industry."[4]

Their business has not always been atop the waters, however. And the story of how it grew, thrived, almost sank, and then came back to become once more a premier boat business actually began in two garages in a little New Hampshire village.

Notes

1. Estimates range from 13 million to 16 million water-skiers, and more than 1.7 million new skiers start each year, according to the American Water Ski Association (AWSA). See "A Profile of Water Skiing in the United States," a brochure of AWSA, June 1996. (In 1997, AWSA became USA Water Ski, moving its headquarters to Polk City, Florida.)
2. "From the Beginning," *The Water Skier,* April 1989, 25.
3. Gregor Ziemer, "Water Skiing's Inventor Recalls Debut on Minnesota Lake in 1922," *Orlando Tribune,* spring/summer 1977. The *Orlando Tribune* was a publication of Correct Craft, the forerunner of *Nautique News.*
4. Jim Harmon, "The Meloons: Three Parts Know-How, Three Parts Faith," *Powerboat,* August 1982, 46.

Chapter 3

The Yankee Boatbuilder

*W*alter C. (W. C.) Meloon was back in town, starting his own business in the little village where he had grown up and met and married Marion Hamm. He bought two garages in Ossipee, New Hampshire, and his mechanical ability and strong work ethic brought him a steady flow of customers. W. C. had developed his natural ability with machines in Buffalo, New York, with jobs at a chemical company, a bridge-making company, and a die-casting company. Now back in Ossipee, the talented mechanic was also rearing three sons at home: Walter O., Ralph, and an infant, Harold. W. C. was confident the business would grow.

Then fire destroyed one garage after a cleaning rag dipped in gasoline ignited. Less than a year later, the second garage burned down when a connected stable and wooden hotel caught fire.

W. C. had limited insurance to cover the losses. It would take five years to fully repay his suppliers, bank, and customers. But pay he did. He worked at the foundry owned by his brother Nat, often pulling two shifts a day. "Dad was a very hard worker and a very fast worker, so he was able to do in two shifts what most people would do in three," reports Ralph. "He was able to save enough money to be able to go back and pay everybody."

W. O. sat in the passenger's seat of the 1924 Dodge sedan as his father drove to the home of the banker's widow to repay the bank loan. "Dad told me what he was doing and why he was doing it," W. O. remembers. "He made it clear to me—and later the family—that until you pay a debt, you still owe it."

W. C. was a Christian but not strong in his faith, and he made no mention of God in his decision to repay. Instead, New England's Puritan principles influenced him, according to his son. "The Puritan religion of that day emphasized repaying your debts," says W. O. "A moral life and honesty were things you had to have. That was something that existed throughout the community, even if you weren't a believer [in Christ]."

Almost thirty years would pass before the next Meloon generation would face similar financial straits and respond with a strong, unwavering commitment to repay its debts, this time motivated by a clear devotion to Christian values that permeated its business.

The Christian faith of W. C. also would become more vigorous. Originally Marion had turned down his marriage proposal, saying she couldn't marry a nonbeliever. "I have become a Christian," he answered her, "and I'll make a public confession as soon as I can." Their local church had closed for lack of a pastor.

Early in their marriage, W. C. fulfilled his spiritual vow. When evangelist Lee Aldrich came to Niagara Falls for a week of meetings, W. C. went forward to make a public commitment. He was baptized, joined the Baptist church, and began to grow in his faith. A week later, he accidentally hammered his thumb and swore. Promptly overwhelmed with guilt and shame, he asked for God's forgiveness. Years later, in intense pain after he caught his hand in an air compressor V-belt and broke a finger, he simply said, "I believe I broke a finger."

W. C. was a wonderful father. With all three sons on his knees, he would tell them bedtime stories about Buffalo Bill and Wild Bill Hickok, always stopping at the height of suspense with a promise to continue the next night.

W. C. loved to tinker with all kinds of machinery. He spent much spare time building a boat powered by a Ford Model T engine driving an old airplane propeller. That hobby set in motion the business that would later catapult his name into the highest ranks of the recreational boating industry. W. C. also built the first tourist cabins in Duncan Lake, New Hampshire. He and Marion sold the lake property in 1925 to move to Florida after persistent urging by two of W. C.'s sisters and a Christian friend, J. Elwyn Wright.

BUILDING BOATS FOR FLORIDA LAKES

In Florida at that time, few boats skimmed the many lakes of the sunshine state. It seemed natural for W. C. to establish the Florida Variety Boat Company, with himself as president. Even the name of the firm allowed plenty of room for experimenting —just what he wanted.

The Yankee invader built his first plant in a central Florida garden spot called Pine Castle, just outside of Orlando. The Florida Variety Boat Company made few ripples in the industry during those early years. But its founder had a flair for promotion, introducing the public to a variety of water sports, all performed behind his powerboats, of course. He often towed his sons in aquaplanes and water skis along the waterfront. The racing engines and rising spray attracted the crowds. They also gave the Meloons valuable public exposure to help sell the boats.

In 1930, the Florida Variety Boat Company became known as the Pine Castle Boat and Construction Company. Eight years later, a radio commercial extolling the virtues of "the correct heel for your shoe" gave W. C. the idea for a new company name. *Great,* he thought. *Why not "the correct craft for you"?* The rest is history. Soon his company began calling its products Correct Craft. The firm was incorporated with that name in 1947.

In spite of her busyness as a mother, Marion still found time to keep the books for the business from its earliest days. She had completed a brief business course and had good business sense. As the children grew old enough to help out at home, she put in many long days at the office without pay. Not until World War II did she agree to accept a modest salary.

During the early thirties, depression stalked the nation and began to take its toll on the boating industry. Three bank failures cost the Meloons all they had. After the second failure, the company sold a dozen boats to officials at Lake Placid, Florida, a tourist attraction 100 miles south of Orlando. The buyers would pay only a token down payment. After repeated attempts to get the money owed them, the Meloons drove to Lake Placid, collected the $300 due, and placed it in a bank on Saturday, along with other small checks they had received. The bank closed down on Monday.

Marion Meloon promptly called all the check writers and asked them to stop payment. The bank had to return the original checks, and their writers wrote new ones. Marion's quick thinking salvaged something from a potential disaster.

BUSY HANDS DURING DEPRESSION TIMES

As the Pine Castle Boat *and* Construction Company, W. C. kept the firm going with key construction jobs. He showed the designer's touch in several projects in Orlando during the 1930s. "We were not making it in the boatbuilding business," Ralph admits. "Construction was a key part of keeping Correct Craft in money through the difficult '30s." W. C. designed and built a system of canals. He also built sturdy boathouses throughout the community that could resist mighty winds, particularly hurricanes that could sweep in from the Caribbean. Before the Meloon boathouses, "every hurricane that came would topple boathouses into the lake," Ralph recalls. W. C. solved the problem by sinking pylons from the base of the sand to the top of the boathouse's eaves. He proudly advertised "storm-proof boathouses" and, in fact, never lost a boat home to a summer storm.

When Orlando wanted to develop Sanlando Spring, W. C. bid and won the project. Located halfway between Sanford and

Orlando, Sanlando Spring was a large spring with plenty of potential, and W. C. built a dam there for long-term water storage and recreational slides for children. The thirty-foot-tall slides dropped squealing kids (and many adults) into the water and were a popular attraction for almost thirty years before water parks such as Orlando's Wet 'n Wild appeared.

To build the dam, W. O. constructed a cofferdam, a temporary watertight enclosure built in the water and pumped dry to expose the spring's bottom. There he and the work crew assembled the actual dam. "He built the dam, the cofferdam, and all the slides," Ralph recalls. "He was a natural at those things."

When Orlando's most successful architect in the 1930s found that his home had a building flaw, he decided to call the expert, W. C. "Mr. Meloon, my house is sinking, and my walls are falling apart," he said. "Can you help me?"

He explained that his home was sinking to the ground without proper pilings to anchor it in the soft central-Florida earth. His mansion had been built along the lakefront, but cracks were appearing in the walls, and water was eroding the ground. Though W. C. was most known as a boatbuilder, the architect knew that the president of the Pine Castle Boat and Construction Company was also a gifted mechanical engineer. He had seen Meloon's handiwork throughout Florida in the canals, boathouses, and dams he had built.

W. C. welcomed the challenge. He began by installing a concrete wall along the beachfront to keep the soft ground and mud from moving toward the lake. To build it, he dug eighteen feet down till he hit hard, dry earth.

Then he went under the house to stabilize the foundation. He assembled four-foot sections of cement pylons and sent them down about twelve feet until he hit hardpan, the compacted earth beneath the water table. W. C. "dug" his way with a water jet—a tapering pipe that channeled high-pressure water spray, clearing the mud and earth easily until it finally struck the hard clay and could excavate no more. After W. C. had blown open this hole, he slipped in the pylon, about two feet from the house. He did this with several pylons, and then he lifted a corner of the house and added wedges. Over a couple of months, W. C. slowly raised the structure and saved the home.

Years later, as Correct Craft was building assault boats for the military, W. C. showed his creative mechanical mind when he devised a unique rescue plan for a downed airliner. A National Airlines plane had overshot the runway in Lakeland, Florida, and rested in a lake just beyond. Three people died; the others escaped and were picked up by boaters. But frustrated rescuers were unable to lift the Lockheed airplane from the lake's bottom. A nephew living in Lakeland called W. C. and explained that the shoreline cranes were unable to reach the plane. "Walt, they can't get it out of the middle of the lake," he said. "Can you figure how to pick that airplane up?"

"Yeah. I'll get it out of there," he said confidently.

He thought of the extra M2 assault boats left in inventory from a recent government project. The military had several purposes for this versatile wood boat. But one seemed especially helpful here: They sometimes linked a dozen or more together, put a tread across their tops, and then ferried goods across this floating platform. Thus they moved people and even trucks across waterways. Each boat could support 5,000 pounds.

W. C. explained his plan to local officials, who gave their approval. He surrounded the plane with four large assault-boat platforms, each made of several boats linked together. Then he sent a diver into the lake to hook four cables onto the plane at a point recommended by Lockheed. A four-foot-wide winch held the end of each cable, and slowly the crews began to turn the four winches. The plane weighed less in the water than on dry ground, and with the four platforms working together, the cables wound around the winches and the plane rose to the surface, until the wings appeared under the platforms. W. C. then started the outboard engine on one platform and gently tugged the plane to shore, where cranes could hoist it onto the sand.

"It was as easy as anything," Ralph recalls, "no problem. . . . Dad could do anything. He just figured how to get a job done at a reasonable cost. Dad always said, 'A mechanic is not a mechanic who can get the job done. A mechanic is one who can get it done without a million dollars' worth of tools.'"

Innovative design and promotion would be hallmarks of the company that years later would build the first tournament ski boat. During his early years in Florida, the founder would enter his boats in local races and win them all. His secret was his propeller with small blades to power what were called "pumpkin seed boats." The outboard engine had not been tinkered with. But his brother Nat used his Syracuse, New York, foundry to build "a propeller more effective than any other," according to W. O.

Innovation also meant revenue from other sources. In 1931, during the heart of the Depression, members of the Meloon family raised money by giving boat rides. Ralph, at age twelve, began taking company boats to nearby lakes to bring in a little money for groceries and help keep the struggling firm afloat.

BOAT RIDES FOR TWENTY-FIVE CENTS

Walt and two of his cousins, Fred and Bud Jones, helped in the beginning. Later his Uncle Cal and one of the firm's employees joined Ralph, and they began to make longer trips. The crew traveled from town to town in search of business, announcing the boat rides by loudspeaker in the town square.

"Only ten and twenty-five cents!" they shouted.

Then they would drive to a nearby lake, launch a boat, and wait for customers. Later, the family put two cars on the road and began to use larger boats, thus attracting larger crowds.

The Meloons' greatest promotion, then as now, would be waterskiing, and they participated in the beginnings of both show skiing and competitive (tournament) skiing. In fact, the publisher of *Powerboat* magazine recently affirmed the Meloons' influence on the sport: "The Meloon/Correct Craft name is known to just about anyone who's interested in water-skiing."[1]

In the beginning, though, waterskiing was not the sole feature of the shows. Two years after the boat business began in Pine Castle, "Dad started towing gliders behind his boats," Ralph remembers. "We used freeboards, aquaplanes, water skis—all kinds of contraptions."

The Meloons often staged shows on Lake Ivanhoe, which remained Orlando's prime site for ski tournaments through the 1980s. They also put on water-ski shows across the Deep South and up the East Coast. The shows attracted buyers to their developing inboard ski boats and eventually the attention of another promoter, Dick Pope.

HELPING CYPRESS GARDENS TO PART THE WATERS

At his modest lake resort in Winter Haven, near Orlando, Pope introduced waterskiing to the local public as early as 1930. It was simply a novelty then, not an organized sport. For five years, Pope presented ski shows, and then he found a piece of property on nearby Lake Eloise that offered an ideal setting for an expanded ski show and a whole lot more. Five years later, he would found Cypress Gardens, home of the first permanently located water-ski show, set amid gorgeous gardens and exhibits. Today there's a unique antebellum village, a natural wildlife preserve, the largest model railroad exhibit in Florida, and a series of shows involving alligators, magic, and performing birds. Visitors also can ride on the Island in the Sky, rotating 153 feet above the ground, for a spectacular view of the surrounding area.

Before Cypress Gardens opened, Ralph joined the venture in a special way. "Dick used to hire me," says Ralph, "to drive him and prospective investors from Winter Haven's Lake Howard through back waterways to Lake Eloise, the current heart of Cypress Gardens. I was only a teenager, and I didn't realize at the time the significance of those excursions." The setting seemed ideal for skiing. Lake Eloise had a clubhouse and a larger building that could be used for headquarters. Behind the buildings and connected to Lake Eloise by a canal was a smaller lake with a jump and slalom course. Though the small Lake Summit was eyed as a great training course for skiers, years later it would also host many successful ski tournaments.

Pope also received help from the U. S. government to develop the land. Ralph again was at the helm of a Correct Craft boat, this time leading officials from Washington on a trip through the Winter Haven chain of lakes to Lake Eloise. "Dick Pope would sit in the middle of the boat as we were slowly coasting around the Cypress Gardens area and back into the canal to Lake Summit, telling his guests what he planned on doing. When he finished his sales pitch, he convinced the Works Progress Administration to furnish the labor to start the gardens."

The first boat Dick bought from W. C. was only a simple rowboat to fish in the lake. Cost: fifty dollars. But when Pope opened the park, he bought all his ski boats from Correct Craft. Years later, Correct Craft boats shared top billing with the Cypress Garden skiers and swimmer/actress Esther Williams in the movie *Easy to Love.* Ten Correct Craft towboats sped across Lake Eloise, and in a memorable scene, Williams skied past a Florida-shaped pool built near the lakeshore.

For almost fifty years, Correct Craft was the exclusive boat of Cypress Gardens. Interestingly, W. C. Meloon never had a written agreement with Dick Pope, so trusting was their relationship. Pope later was installed in the Water Ski Hall of Fame.

Correct Craft boats continued to gain prominence as recreational craft. At Cypress Gardens, Jordan's King Hussein water-skied for the first time behind a twenty-foot Correct Craft Tournament Skier. He liked the boat so well that he later bought four Correct Craft boats for his own use. He and the royal family continue to purchase boats today, about one every other year.

HARD WORK

Behind the glamour of having boats next to movie stars and kings was plenty of hard work. It was not uncommon to find W. C.'s shirts and ties scattered around the plant where he had removed them to perform some task.

On one occasion, his wife phoned Correct Craft executive Norman Sewell to alert him. "Will you watch out for some bankers who are coming to the plant today?" she asked. "We're anxious to make a good impression so we can get a loan. Be sure to see that Dad is properly dressed when they come."

When the bankers arrived, they began to ask questions about W. C. Sewell thought it best to pave the way for whatever they might find. "If you see someone with his sleeves rolled up," he suggested, "that will probably be Mr. Meloon."

But they still didn't expect to see a grease-covered man lifting a boat. Fortunately, what they saw impressed them. Not every firm had its president pitching in to do even the dirtiest work.

W. C. expected the same attitude from his workers. They stood as they built boats. "Even if someone could do the job quicker sitting down, he wanted the person to stand," Ralph says. "If you could do the job quicker sitting down, he didn't like that. He believed people should be on their toes all the time."

"I worked with him day in and day out," says truck driver Slim Guntrie. "He never asked an employee to do anything he wouldn't do himself. And he always had time to say a cheery word to you no matter where you were. When he was intent on business, nothing else mattered—his clothes or his own well-being.

"One cold December day, we were putting in a boat dock on a lake. He drove the car right down to the edge of the water, then walked out into the water in his good clothes, up to his waist, showing me where the dock should go."

KINDNESS AND CHARACTER

W. C.'s abilities as a mechanic and his devotion to work did not make him indifferent to his workers. He believed everyone should be treated fairly. *Honesty* and *equal treatment* were his watchwords. That extended to the home as well. "If I and someone were sitting in a room talking about another person who was not present, and my grandfather was there, he would stand up and walk out of the room," recalls W. N. Meloon, current president of Correct Craft. "He'd not listen to the conversation. He would not be a party to that. He wanted you to go and talk to the person."

W. C. also refused to acknowledge anyone as his enemy. When a man with a real or imagined grievance avoided him on the sidewalk one day as they passed, W. C. walked briskly around the block. He confronted his "enemy" again and engaged him in friendly conversation. Competitors and creditors found it impossible to remain angry with him. He possessed a calmness and serenity that surprised and sometimes frustrated his friends.

"Dad was a lover of people," says Harold, the youngest son. "I just don't know anyone who didn't think very highly of my father. Most everyone had nothing but a good word for Dad."

Much of his kindness developed with his Christian faith, which his sons say grew with his friendship with the pastor of the local church, O. G. Hall. The Baptist minister and W. C. spent hours talking about spiritual matters and church business.

Under the pastor's wise counsel, W. C. became convinced the Lord would help him pay his bills if he worked only six days a week instead of seven. Accordingly, he set the company policy to prohibit Sunday work (as the army would later learn). Soon he found himself able to pay not only his own bills, but also Pastor Hall's college debt.

Harold remembers his father initially working on Sundays to pay bills: "He'd say, 'If you owe someone something, you should keep the doors open on Sunday.'" But after hearing the pastor's message on honoring the Lord's Day, Harold says, "he immediately put signs up reading 'No work on the Lord's Day.'" That change had to please Marion. The boat factory was located just across from their Baptist church. Some Sundays she found herself teaching the adult women's class over the roar of outboard engines being tested. "Mother used to really complain about that," Harold says with a chuckle. The policy of no Sunday work has remained in place ever since.

DEVOTION TO GOD

Prayer became a natural part of W. C.'s lifestyle, and he was not ashamed of his Christian beliefs among his colleagues. That was especially evident in 1951, when union men tried to organize the Correct Craft plant in Titusville. Correct Craft had opened this second plant fifty miles east of Pine Castle on the Atlantic Coast during World War II. The Titusville plant had met military demand for boats, and now, with peace and stability, labor unions wanted to organize.

At the time, Max K. Aulick operated both the Southern Lighting Manufacturing Company and the Orlando Boat Company. His firms made gas tanks for Correct Craft boats and helped to manufacture some components for the first military aluminum bridge-erection boats, also built by the Meloons. During meetings with the union men, Aulick noticed that they had suddenly discontinued their efforts to organize Correct Craft.

"Why did you drop Correct Craft?" he asked.

"Do you want to know the truth?" responded the union negotiator.

"Yes," Aulick said.

"Every time we went over there and started a meeting to discuss negotiations, W. C. Meloon insisted on praying before the discussion began." The union organizer got so tired of the praying that he decided to forget the whole thing.

Eager to see everyone have faith in Jesus Christ, W. C. looked for ways to share a natural witness with family and business contacts. In 1943, he conducted his first chapel service. They have continued to this day, making Correct Craft a pioneer in industrial evangelism.[2]

In fact, one of Correct Craft's distinguishing features is that it attempts to run its entire business "by the Book"—the Bible.

Notes

1. Jerry Nordskog, "Letter from the Publisher," *Powerboat,* December 1994, 4.
2. The Meloons followed the lead of industrialist R. G. LeTourneau in having a chapel time at work, according to W. O. Meloon.

Chapter 4
Working by the Book

*M*ore than fifty years after Correct Craft produced its "miracle boats" for General Eisenhower, the family's management continues to adhere to Christian principles in its daily operations. The Meloons desire to honor God and run their boat business by His Word, the Bible. Working by the Book means consulting the Scriptures and spending time in prayer. Until his death in 1974, W. C. spent time on his knees beside his bed each evening. When burdens troubled him during the night, he arose and prayed until the Lord satisfied him that everything was all right.

The second president, Ralph Meloon (1955–1960), prayed so often during one company crisis that his knees swelled, and a doctor had to withdraw a pint of fluid from the inflamed knees. When Ralph explained he had been on his knees praying, the doctor prescribed a sturdy pillow. Ralph still spends extended time each morning in prayer. The third president, Walt. O. (1960–1984), and his son and current president, W. N., couple prayer with notable Christian service. The National Association of Evangelicals once named W. O. its Man of the Year for his efforts in organizing and leading Christian relief efforts following the 1976 Guatemala earthquake. W. N. serves on governing boards guiding a home for abused girls, House of Hope, and a private Christian school, the Hampden-DuBose Academy.

Although working by the Book still means observing a day of rest on Sunday, it means a lot more in terms of attitudes and actions. "The strong Christian beliefs which permeate the family's professional as well as personal lives have gained the respect and admiration of their peers," a reporter once wrote in an industry magazine. "One hears such terms as 'honesty,' 'character' and 'integrity' in descriptions of the Meloons."[1] To the Meloons, faith coupled with vision make perfect business sense.

THE MISSION OF CORRECT CRAFT

What should be the mission of a company founded on Christian principles? According to W. N. Meloon, Correct Craft's goal is "to build boats for the glory of God, as very simply stated by my grandfather, Walter C. Meloon." In businesses where the owners or top executives aren't Christians, the goal is "to make money, to be profitable," according to W. N. Making a profit is important at Correct Craft as well, but it's not "the most important thing."

"My job is to make money. There's no doubt about it," W. N. says. "My job is to protect the investment of the stockholders, and I work at that every day. But I can't forget the other things that are even more important. God gave me another mission, and that is to do today whatever I do for the glory of Him. All this that is on my desk has got to be done at the same time. It's got to move along and be done in the proper time and with the proper attitude. And in doing so, there are a lot of other things that happen. One of those is that you've got to remember those who help you complete that task, the employees."

Other groups and individuals draw the company's attention, too, including its suppliers, bankers, and government agencies. "For the glory of God and to fulfill our responsibilities to these key groups, Correct Craft continually strives to increase its financial base," W. N. explains.

In an earlier history of the company, W. N. emphasized the consistency of Correct Craft's purpose: It "has not changed, neither will it change from that of producing quality recreational boats and servicing our customers at a profit as a means of glorifying God and rendering Him excellent. . . . The business principles, ethics, and morals of Correct Craft [come] through God's strength and enable us to stand strong, unyielding to mediocrity."[2]

W. N. believes the company's founder, as a Christian business owner, recognized that hard work and a reasonable profit would honor God. "My grandfather used to say, 'If a job is worth doing, it's worth doing right' and 'We'll do the impossible first, and all the rest will be taken care of.'" Though clichés, those sayings remind W. N. that work, profit, and honoring God can complement each other. And the eleven-member board of directors embraces that mission statement, he notes. "All our board members are Christians. They also come from a world that in many cases is very secular, because they work for people who are not Christians. So they see a mission statement such as 'We're going to build the finest product there is, and we're going to sell it for the best price.' We accomplish all those things, but we want to do it to the glory of God."

STABLE POLICIES

The company's consistent Christian stand through the years has given employees a standard on which they count. Among many stable policies, two stand out as part of a strong Christian statement of belief: no work on Sunday, and no alcohol at business gatherings.

When a prospective manager is being interviewed, the president outlines the corporate policy. "I tell our managers when they come to work here that this is a Christian family business," W. N. says. "There are things we do and things we don't do. We don't buy alcohol for meetings, and we don't drink alcohol. We don't do business over alcohol. We don't work on Sunday."

One exception exists to the no-work-on-Sunday policy, and that's to help others in an industry that can be very busy during ski tournament weekends. As a strong supporter of professional water-ski tournaments, the company makes its representatives available to help when Correct Craft boats are operating as official towboats in tournaments.

If an event is underway on a Sunday, "and our product breaks down, and we refuse to fix it or to help them because it's a Sunday, they will reject this 'religion thing' of the company," W. N. explains. "There are a few Sundays that we have to work, because the people would not understand if we didn't. But if I have to schedule work on every Sunday, then my heart and my intent are wrong."

Still, in an industry where boat shows typically continue through the weekends, Correct Craft sales representatives won't be there on Sundays. The shows mean direct sales to dealers and both immediate and future sales to customers, so Correct Craft reps will be at the show through Saturday. But on Saturday night, the company employee returns to his hotel room and won't be back on the job until Monday morning. "Now, if the employee doesn't have anything to do when he's in Chicago and he wants to walk around the show and look, that's fine," W. N. notes. "But he is not to go in the booth and work."

The policy has caused some lost business, W. N. admits. On occasion, some company reps have complained about lost opportunities. "We simply tell them that as Christians, we follow the example God set," W. N. says. "He took a day of rest, and we believe we should also take a day of rest and honor Him by worship and other things."

Employees at a boat show may even explain the policy to a prospective customer. When a boat show runs Thursday through Sunday, for instance, someone may say, "I might come back later this weekend; can I see you Sunday afternoon?"

The answer is professional and can even become a positive statement about the company: "Well, this is a Christian family business, and we don't work on Sundays. We take Sundays off and go to church. If we can do something on Saturday, fine. If not, here's my business card. Give me a call on Monday. We can close this deal then, no problem."

This observance of the Lord's Day does not mean a person must be a Christian to work at Correct Craft. Many employees aren't. The non-Christians throughout the company offer good ideas and add a dimension to the work that keeps the Meloons and other believers at the company sharp in their faith.

If the company hired only Christians, what would happen to ministry, W. N. wonders. "If I surround myself with Christians, what kind of challenge is there for me to be an example all day long?"

Sometimes prospective employees have heard of the business's Christian beliefs and write W. N. praising the company. "I would just love to work for a Christian company," they typically say. "I need to get out of this godless company I'm in." Though he doesn't rule out their eventually coming to Correct Craft, W. N. says that "the first thing I do is write back and say, 'Have you ever thought that maybe God has you in that godless company for a reason?'"

Even some managers at the company are not Christians. But W. N. insists that before they join Correct Craft, they must be willing to be "ethically and morally correct, and they must accept the principles and the ethics of this family and this company. And that's a challenge I tell them right out front."

W. N. desires as managers "people who may not agree with the directions I take. . . . For half the price, I could go out and get a bunch of sheep to come in here and say, 'Yes sir; yes, sir; yes, sir.' When they agree with the decision and the direction I'm taking, I want their full support. When they disagree with it, I want them to stand up and throw the flag."

When that happens, the manager and president will have a dialogue. If they still can't come to an agreement, "we'll take it into the management group and say, 'Guys, is he right and you just haven't come forward to support him? Where are we in this thing?'"

SUPPORT FOR CHRISTIAN VALUES

The company's non-Christian managers support its values because they can see that the principles make good business sense, and that they must be loyal to the company. "It's something individually that each manager and myself have got to commit ourselves to," W. N. explains. "You can have group meetings all you want, but if you don't have the individual commitment, and he's not committed in his heart, forget that meeting; it's not going to work.

"Anytime I interview a new manager, I make it very plain what the Meloons are. We're born-again Christians. Period. Secondly, we're boatbuilders. I say, 'If you don't believe in the policies of this company, or in the principles and ethics we practice in this company, you're going to have to learn to conform to them.'" If they're not willing, the president knows they can't help the company meet its mission of glorifying God in the production of boats.

The company has made many contributions to waterskiing and recreational boating with its advances and innovations. But remaining a leader in the water-ski industry in the twenty-first century will require more than offering new technologies, W. N. believes. Correct Craft must remain true to its mission.

"As businessmen and boatbuilders, we've got to strive as always to go to better products and to service our customers better," he says. "That's pretty plain. But one of the most important challenges of the future will be from a spiritual standpoint. Can we continue to build boats to honor God and His Word? And in doing so, can we make a profit?"

HELPING CAMPS AND ORGANIZATIONS

Working by the Book for the Meloons means many other things as well (see chapters 7, 8, and 13 in particular). Perhaps the most important is giving back to God as He blesses you. The Meloons strongly believe that everything they have—from their health to their skills and business profits—comes from God and should be returned to Him. They believe they are stewards, and they give generously of their resources. One of the most notable ways they do this is by providing ski boats at a nominal charge to Christian camps and organizations that will use the craft for ministry.

The company's flagship model, the Ski Nautique, skims the lakes at Christian camps operated by Young Life, Wheaton College, and Word of Life, among others. At Camp Joy in Whitewater Lake, Wisconsin, three Ski Nautiques run all summer, and the results please Correct Craft executives. "They were not able to reach many teens above age thirteen until they got the boats," says Ralph Meloon, now chairman of the Correct Craft board of directors. "These kids are too sophisticated to just play volleyball at camp. Something fast, like a boat and waterskiing, will attract them. When they see a Ski Nautique there, they will come. We're getting older teenagers—sixteen, seventeen, eighteen—in there and seeing them saved in these camps."

In the Correct Craft Christian camp program, the camp staff can buy a boat from a dealer at the wholesale price. Then Correct Craft gives the dealer a check for $1,000 for selling the boat. "The dealer doesn't make much, so we limit it," Ralph says. "We make sure they're a *Christian* camp."

Because the camps work directly with Correct Craft dealers, however, new business can be generated for those dealers. The boats at summer camps get rave reviews that catch the attention of parents and friends who may be thinking of buying a ski boat for themselves.

Camp directors see the impact of the program. Correct Craft first provided a ski boat at Camp Gilead, Florida, in 1975. Now the camp receives a replacement boat every two years. "What an addition to the camp program of reaching young people for Christ and providing them with a fun time while here!" wrote camp director Edith Hulslander. "Waterskiing is a favorite activity, and many attend camp because of it. Driving the boat every afternoon is my special fun time, and it is great to see the campers enjoying it so much."[3]

A few boats are given away free of charge. Correct Craft

donates one or two a year; some are given to colleges that need
boats for their ski teams. These are used boats in excellent condition, typically from a ski school, a ski tournament—or even
from Sea World (which uses Ski Nautique boats exclusively)—
that has sold the boat back to Correct Craft after limited use.
The boats have few miles logged (actually "hours" in boating
terms) and have been maintained well by the original user.

Through the years, the company has also donated boats to
missionaries.

The company's policy of giving back to God from all you
have traces its roots to a time when Correct Craft lost almost
everything. When the losses came, the Meloons knew God was
still faithful, and they still lived by the Book and spent the next
twenty-five years working their way back to financial wholeness.
It remains the most compelling story of the company's trust in
biblical principles. Many people say that here—when a dishon-
est inspector nearly destroyed Correct Craft—is where the
words *honesty, character,* and *integrity* were first widely
applied to the Meloons.

Notes

1. Jim Harmon, "The Meloons: Three Parts Know-How, Three Parts Faith," *Power-boat,* August 1982, 46.
2. Robert G. Flood, *On the Waters of the World* (Chicago: Moody, 1989), 9.
3. "Letters," *Nautique News,* spring/summer 1994, 3.

Chapter 5

Up from the Waters

*L*ike many companies, Correct Craft rode a golden wave in the 1950s. The peacetime economy was generating jobs, people felt good about the future, and families were expanding, creating a baby boom. Correct Craft now was making fifty-foot yachts, fishing boats, and, of course, ski boats. It continued to win contracts from a military that was well aware of the company's reputation for reliability after the "miracle boats" that stormed the Rhine.

The future looked even brighter in 1957 when the boat-builder received a government contract for three thousand boats. Production began smoothly on the fiberglass assault boats. Then one day, the chief of a three-man inspection team asked to meet with W. O. and Ralph.

"Did you know," he asked, "that you're one of only two companies in the whole Southeast that don't have someone on their payroll who carries an expense account to take care of the inspectors' expenses?"

"No, I didn't," answered W. O., then the sales manager. He was feeling his way carefully. He knew the government took care of such expenses itself and that the question was a veiled request for a payoff through double reimbursement. He also knew that the man across the table, as chief inspector for eight southeastern states, held major influence and power.

The inspector's business smile now seemed rather grim. His sullen look made the Correct Craft officers uneasy. "I wondered if he really had misspoken," recalls Ralph, who sat next to the inspector, across from W. O. "The contract clearly said no gratuities. We couldn't even give an inspector a Coca-Cola or cup of coffee."

It sounded like a payoff scheme. But *bribe, payoff,* and *slush fund* were not part of the Meloon vocabulary. The Meloon brothers said nothing.

THE REJECTED ASSAULT BOATS

More than 2,000 boats had already been assembled and accepted by the government. Within two weeks, though, the inspection team had begun to find "flaws" that were fatal to the boats. Uneven surfaces, poor finishes, and numerous minor defects were reported, making scores of boats unacceptable to the inspectors. Ralph, then president, watched as the stacks of rejected boats grew. He summoned his brother. "Those government people are rejecting an awful lot of boats," he said.

"Well," W. O. replied, "we don't want to deliver anything that isn't right."

"True," Ralph said, "but tiny blemishes are clearly allowable under terms of the contract."

The high rate of rejections continued. At one point, eight of every ten boats were disapproved, Ralph remembers. After building more than four hundred assault boats one decade earlier and receiving the military's high commendation, Correct Craft suddenly watched scores of its assault boats being rejected.

Then Correct Craft tried an experiment. Selecting one of the rejected boats, they cleaned off the inspector's chalk marks and sent it back through the line on a later shift. This time it passed inspection.

The silent war continued. At times the Meloons thought, *Why not pay the man off? It really isn't much compared to what the company stands to lose.* Their father, W. C., had retired two years earlier. They remembered his policy as president: "If you have made a decision based only on money, you have made a bad decision."

W. C. wavered only slightly when his sons told him of the inspectors' tactics. "Dad was tempted," W. O. says. "The bribe didn't amount to much compared with what we stood to lose. But he knew it wasn't right."[1]

Ralph agreed, and W. O. settled the issue one night as he lay awake "wrestling with the problem." He left his bed and knelt on the living room floor, his open Bible on a stool before him.

There he prayed and studied the Scriptures. "The Lord led me through His Word," he says. "In the light of my living room lamp, these words seemed to glow: 'Trust in the Lord with all thine heart; and lean not unto thine own understanding. In all thy ways acknowledge him, and he shall direct thy paths'" (Proverbs 3:5-6, KJV).

"That had to be our answer," W. O. says today. "To pay off the man would not be trusting the Lord but, rather, giving in to the devious ways of the world."

Many boats were being approved, but the rejections continued, even increasing in number. Workers were now stacking rejected boats in the storage yard. At one point, W. O. wondered if the Lord had forgotten them. Reading the Bible, he expressed his concern that night in prayer. An inner voice responded, *"Have you forgotten the storm boats and what I did for you then?"*

The family decided it would do what it could, short of dishonesty, to satisfy the government. By year's end, the firm had delivered 2,200 approved boats. But 600 rejects remained in the storage yard.

Then came the final blow. A railroad flatcar had just been loaded with forty previously passed boats. The chief inspector suddenly appeared just as the switch engine backed up to the flatcar. He turned to W. O. and said, pointing to the boats, "I don't like their looks. They've got to be unloaded and refinished."

That arbitrary decision, unfair as it was, made it impossible to continue. The contract already had cost the company $1 million more than it had received, and Correct Craft now owed half a million dollars to 228 creditors. They filed a complaint with the Army Corps of Engineers in an attempt to collect on expenses owed them under their contract (you can't sue the government), but to no avail. Also, the bank had withdrawn all its commitments.

At a special meeting, the creditors heard the full story. Correct Craft promised to pay them as soon as possible and asked for suggestions.

One creditor recommended that the firm seek protection under chapter 11 of the Bankruptcy Act, which allows management to continue in the interest of creditors. Others agreed to that implicit vote of confidence in the Meloon integrity, and in August 1958, that step was taken. The Meloons were allowed to pay ten cents on the dollar to clear their debts, reorganize, and continue business. But how could they build boats without money?

A TIME FOR SACRIFICE

Management and employees took prudent steps. Every employee agreed to resign, and Ralph and W. O. rehired only those with essential jobs. Ralph's wife, Betty, worked the switchboard for a while. Later W. O.'s wife, Ann, took over. Sometimes she was able to answer questions or clear up misunderstandings without disturbing W. O. Other times she found out the nature of the call and alerted W. O. so he could take a moment to pray for wisdom before answering.

W. O. returned his new Lincoln to the dealer and drove the old company pickup. Other family members sold their cars as well, some choosing to walk to work.

W. C. and Marion never went to court during the bankruptcy proceedings. Their sons chose to spare them the ordeal.

But they could not escape the harassment day after day from anxious creditors. The family waited upon God for a solution.

"Our first answer," W. O. says with characteristic candor, "was a gift of enough guts to get up and face the situation each day. And that was no small victory. God didn't give us comfort at that time, but He did give faith enough to face the next morning."

FRIENDS, FAMILY, AND PAKISTAN

Creditors were pressing the company. And then, as the Meloons considered reorganizing under bankruptcy, three events showed the power of friends, family, and, the Meloons say, a faithful God, who used a foreign government to bless the company.

First, a Norwegian business friend, Torrey Mosvold, loaned money to Correct Craft to provide needed capital and help repay some of the creditors. The boat magnate headed Mosvold Shipping Company and had met the Meloons at one of their business breakfasts held during a New York boat show. Each year, Correct Craft had sponsored a free breakfast for those in the boating industry, followed by a message from an evangelist. Mosvold, a Christian and friend of Correct Craft comptroller Gus Gustafson, attended, met the Meloons, and heard evangelist Jack Wyrtzen address the crowd. He trusted these men who ran their company by Christian principles.

Second, W. O. devised a plan to sell boats outside their Florida base with minimal start-up costs. They would open distribution outlets in New Hampshire, New Jersey, and Indiana. Thus began New England, Mid-Atlantic, and Midwest Correct Craft, and a warehouse system that still exists. But each distribution center needed $10,000 in capital, and the headquarters had little money to lend.

Here came friends and family to the rescue again. Dave Chambers, a friend and businessman, contributed money and began Mid-Atlantic. Betty Meloon leaned over her fence one day and told a neighbor of the plans to open a center in the Midwest, and the neighbor loaned them the money. And their father,

W. C., excited about an opportunity to help, contributed $5,100 from his own savings and from a brother-in-law to start the New England sales office. Once again, W. C. and Marion were in the boating business. From those three points, this new sales force visited dealers locally and hundreds of miles distant, winning boat orders. Ralph resigned from the presidency and hit the road for Illinois and later Indiana, while W. O. assumed the presidency.

Third, the Pakistani government placed an order for more than two hundred of the assault boats sitting in the factory. That amazing order came after a retired Pakistani army major wrote asking for a price quotation on boats like those Correct Craft had built for the U. S. Army in 1951. The U. S. government, it seems, had given some of those boats to Pakistan.

At first, the Meloons filed the letter away unanswered. The handwritten letter was unassuming, and with limited funds, why visit Pakistan for a probable small order?

But Major Moodi Farouki sent a second letter, this time asking, "Would you please do me the courtesy of answering my previous correspondence?"

Perhaps embarrassed, W. O. replied immediately. That began a flurry of correspondence that culminated in a $139,000 contract from the government of Pakistan. The Meloons had no money to make new assault boats, but more than 600 quality fiberglass boats, with slight or no blemishes, were available. Correct Craft shipped one to Pakistan's minister of defense as a sample, with the notice that many others were ready to ship.

An order came back for 239 of the rejected boats. Pakistan signed two contracts, including one for six larger boats.

Several days later, though, Farouki called W. O. at home; it was 3 A.M. Pakistan was canceling the contracts, he announced. "The U. S. government has sent a man over here to tell our minister of defense that you people are not honorable," he explained, "and that we should not do business with you."

W. O. thought a moment before he replied. "Well, Moodi," he said, trying to hear the distant voice, "I can't answer all your questions by phone, but I'll be glad to correspond further with you."

The next morning, W. O. received a telegram confirming the cancellation. He and the rest of the family reeled from shock. Both the comptroller and treasurer were upset and wanted to stop production on the boats.

"I told them we were not going to stop," W. O. says. "We had committed the bidding process on these boats to the Lord. We had even passed up the first two bid dates and submitted our bid on a third and final date, at Pakistan's insistence. I felt God had intervened."

Now they would once more trust God. Unknown to them, the Pakistani government decided to reinstate the contract for the six larger boats, even as Correct Craft had reinspected and was ready to test the first boat. But the reinstatement notice failed to arrive in the mail. Still, W. O. decided to send ten smaller boats, also tested and approved, with the first large boat, hoping Pakistan would accept them.

"Ten days later, we received the checks for all eleven boats," W. O. reports.

"We continued to ship truckload after truckload, as the boats were finished. Back came the checks, with no protest. In time, the Pakistan embassy paid for all 239 of the boats they had originally requested."

As a result, the company enjoyed a new lease on life. But there were still those early-morning calls from creditors. "I learned much from those experiences," W. O. says. "By no means were all the financial problems solved, but by this time we had learned to relax and trust God. A few years previously, I would have found it difficult to spend fifteen minutes at a time in prayer. Now I was spending up to an hour or more each day on my knees. We continued to work and to pay a few more creditors as the cash flow allowed."

Other friends offered help. Bud Coleman, owner of a local automobile agency, granted Correct Craft a ten-year loan on the plant property, and when the Meloons finally could pay it off,

Coleman refused to compound the interest. He had simply added each yearly amount of interest to the principle. Correct Craft was amazed.

And A. B. Johnson, founder of Orlando's best-known electrical firm and an associate in the Christian Businessmen's Committee of Orlando, submitted a very low bid to wire one of Correct Craft's warehouses. He not only wired the building at a nominal cost, but he also was now entitled to attend the creditors' meetings. Often none of the Meloons was invited to the meetings, and Johnson looked after their best interests. His wise counsel over a period of many months kept the Meloon family from being forced out of the firm's management. A. B. Johnson was completely blind, yet he played golf and shot in the eighties on local courses; he became "the blind Samaritan" for the Meloons.

LIFE ON THE ROAD

As W. O. learned more lessons about trust at company headquarters, Ralph was learning similar lessons on the road. He had left the presidency and would live in tents and prefabricated houses for the next few years.

"Betty was willing to be on the road, live in a tent, and deliver boats with me," he says. "I'd tow boats behind my car, and she'd take one behind her car." The first year they stayed in Aurora, Illinois. Then for two years they had a tent in a campground near Angola. Next they had a Jim Walker house, a simple, prefabricated structure with just the roof, sides, and floor. Inside they had only a mattress and a picnic table given by a friend. They had no water or electricity, but, Ralph notes, "we didn't have to raise a tent when we returned home."

Eventually a local plumber added plumbing, a shower, and a toilet. The Meloons also bought an Underwood typewriter (cost: $10) to prepare invoices. Betty didn't know how to type, but she learned at night school.

During the early camping days, Ralph would demonstrate the boat and leave Betty "home" at the tent. "Can you imagine this wonderful girl?" Ralph marvels as he recalls those days. "She'd stay there and once in a while face thunderstorms alone." When the rains came, the tent got wet, as did the ground, and Betty had to escape to the women's room at the campground—the only place surrounded by cement block and thus dry. That was also her refuge when the other Midwest weather scourge arrived, tornadoes.

"She never complained," Ralph says with admiration. "It was really tough for us materially, but my wife and I were never closer. We had some great times together. I had more time with her then than I had before."

Prior to bankruptcy, Ralph had often flown to bid on government contracts, trying to land a large order. His schedule was hectic during World War II and the Korean War. "I was flying to Pittsburgh, Chicago, New York, and St. Louis," he says. "My wife hardly saw me. The DC-3 plane seemed to take all night to get there." Many weeks, he was away two or three days.

Once he was stationed in Indiana, setting up Midwest Correct Craft, his wife drove with him—as did his sons in the summer—and they spent much more time together. They'd set up the tent within fifty miles of the dealer, and Ralph would make a presentation, returning that evening. His sales territory now spanned 600 miles, as far west as South Dakota. Camping may have gotten into their blood, for since then Ralph and Betty have tent-camped in all forty-nine continental states.

During the midwinters, when the Midwest chill and snow made tent-camping impractical, the Meloons returned to Florida. That meant even more time with his wife, though Ralph would travel north a couple times each winter to present Correct Craft products at boat shows.

ESTABLISHING MIDWEST CORRECT CRAFT

Ralph found firmer footing for Midwest Correct Craft once a friendly dealer in Angola agreed to let Ralph store five boats at his showroom year-round without charge. In return, the dealer could sell the boats each spring, and Ralph would restock the dealership with new boats, not charging for shipping or creating inventory costs. Ralph also installed an electric hoist to help the dealer unload the boats. Their arrangement meant fifty boats a year came through the dealer and the new Midwest "warehouse."

"We had a good deal," Ralph says. "We were about 150 yards from his storage area. Betty and I would walk up a hill to his place. And on Saturdays, when he was busy with customers, I'd often align engines for him and help out his customers at the marina. He did a lot for us, and we did a lot for him."

Now the Meloons had better toilet facilities, a warehouse for storing boats, and even office space. Son Ken helped during summers by moving boats, even driving a tractor with a boat in the rear, to the marina. And at age twelve, Ken became an effective sales tool.

"I'd let him put the boat on the lake and demonstrate," Ralph explains. "The prospective dealers were sold on the fact that if a twelve-year-old could do this, the boat was simple to operate. As I came back up from the lake, I'd see them keep looking back as Ken would load the boat and put it in the warehouse. When he got to be sixteen, we bought him a car, and he started delivering boats."

From pulling Correct Craft boats into marinas at age twelve, Ken has grown up to direct operations at two Correct Craft warehouses, Midwest and Southwest. The Southwest operation is located near Tyler, Texas, in the small town of Lindale.

Ralph Meloon stayed in Indiana operating Midwest Correct Craft for more than fifteen of the twenty-five years the company was in bankruptcy. The former company president views it as a time of great spiritual growth. He also admits that growth came in the midst of bumpy times.

"The hardest thing was when we'd pray and nothing happened right then," he says. "Of course, God's timing is a whole lot better than ours. When we'd pray for hours, sometimes we'd think those prayers weren't getting above the ceiling. During those times, you don't think God's hearing at all. But we didn't have anything else to hang on to. God says, 'You're either going to worship Me or you're going to worship mammon.' Well, we didn't have much money. God kept us poor, and we were learning."

During this bankruptcy-recovery period, Ralph began to better understand the Bible and how to pray. And his faith and that of his brother W. O. grew. "We learned so much of how good God is and how capable He is," Ralph reports.

THE NEXT STEP

While Ralph was on the road, W. O. was trying to repay creditors. Within a year of declaring bankruptcy, Correct Craft had distributed $10,000 in checks. But attorneys for the remaining creditors had filed legal papers for their impatient clients. Those creditors wanted the Meloon family removed from the company's management. This time, loss of the firm seemed imminent.

The day of the hearing in Tampa federal court arrived. A. B. Johnson insisted on riding from Orlando in the car with the Meloons rather than with other members of the creditors' committee. Attorney Jim Welch and company controller Ray White also joined.

On the way to court, the people in the car prayed. "Lord," they said, "we know the charges are largely true. We've made mistakes. We need about forty-five days to get the problems straightened out."

The judge listened to the arguments on both sides and then concluded, "I'll be prepared to hear more on the Correct Craft matter on March 15 in Orlando."

In the car going home, one of the men suddenly thought to count the number of days before the next hearing. They had prayed for forty-five. They now had forty-six!

The day of the next hearing in Orlando arrived. Correct Craft still had no solution to the firm's financial problems. That's why the opening move by the creditors' attorney caught them completely by surprise.

"Judge," he said, "I don't know why, but since the hearing

in Tampa, my clients have asked that I withdraw the com-
plaints." In three minutes, the hearing was over. Another
important skirmish had been won. Yet negotiations dragged on
for six more years. Finally, the judge retired, and the court
appointed a replacement.

He promptly notified the Meloon family that he was going
to liquidate the company in ten days.

By this time, the small creditors had been paid off—101
of them. The remaining 127 creditors had received 10 percent
of what they were owed, but the judge would proceed with liq-
uidation unless they all agreed to a settlement on their remaining balance. W. O. had ten days to convince the creditors
to approve some settlement.

He prepared a letter to those creditors asking a direct question: "Would you accept a settlement of [an additional] 10 percent
from the Meloon family within six months, in lieu of the judge
putting us out of business?" He put it in the day's mail and then
began calling the creditors, explaining that the proposal was
coming and answering any questions.

In nine days, W. O. was able to call 100 creditors. All but
one agreed to his proposal, and the signed letters were
returned to Correct Craft. The judge contacted each creditor on
his own to confirm the consensus. Satisfied, he released Correct Craft from chapter 11 of the Bankruptcy Act on the first
business day of 1965.

THE GOVERNMENT PAYS

A few weeks later, government attorneys for the Corps of
Engineers called Correct Craft's attorney, offering a settlement
of $40,000 to drop its original complaint. W. O. says, "They told
us, 'We [the Corps of Engineers] realized we had some responsibilities, too. This is what you can have. Take this or have
nothing.' They were implying, 'You could go to Congress and
sue us,' but of course, you could not sue an entity of the government."

Correct Craft accepted the $40,000 settlement, which paid

its attorney, as well as his associate in Washington, D. C. The action also caused the Internal Revenue Service to accept the company's claim that the balance of its bills from building the rejected boats, totaling $280,000, was a valid loss. The write-off would allow Correct Craft to operate up to four years without paying any income tax, assuming profits did not exceed $280,000.

After paying attorneys' fees, the balance of the settlement went to the company's creditors. During the six months following the government's offer, Correct Craft actually made three payments totaling 20 percent more of what it owed—twice the additional 10 percent the court had directed. It more than satisfied the law. But as time passed, it still did not satisfy the Meloons.

The Meloons chose to locate and repay all their creditors 100 percent. As they explained to those who ask, "It's the right thing to do." For the next nineteen years, they located and repaid creditors. Once Ralph flew to Michigan to search for a creditor after telephone calls proved fruitless. And when a creditor had died, Correct Craft chose to pay the nearest relative and spent time searching for the person.

FROM THE FISH'S MOUTH

By 1984, Correct Craft had repaid all but $147,000 of its debt. Most of the businesses that had not been paid in full wrote off the balance to bad debt and forgot about it. But at the outset of this particular year, the Meloons vowed with new determination to pay back the rest, even though they didn't know where the money would come from.

"The firm was still operating on borrowed capital, and banks do not make loans to corporations that are losing money," says Ralph. "This meant that each time we paid five thousand dollars to a former creditor, we also had to set aside five thousand dollars for taxes (we were in a 48 percent bracket). So to come out even, we knew we would have to make about $300,000 more than usual in order to pay off the balance and taxes too."

By May 1, they had reduced the debt balance to $50,000.

But with the new 1985 boat models needing funds for retooling by July 1, they knew they had to pay off their debts by June or wait till the next year.

As in previous years, Correct Craft sponsored a bass fishing team to promote its fishing boat, the Bass Nautique. For use of the boat, when the pro fishermen won any prize money, they kept half and gave Correct Craft the other half. No team members had ever won any big money. But in May 1984, during Super Bass III, Nautique member Doug Gilley pulled in more than fifty-three pounds of bass in four days (seven fish per day limit). He won first prize: $100,000. Gilley presented Correct Craft with a check for $50,000, *just enough to pay off the rest of the money it owed creditors.*

Correct Craft and the Meloon family rejoiced and gave thanks to the Lord. And then they remembered a familiar event in the Scriptures. While Jesus was in Capernaum, some of His critics asked Peter, "Doesn't your teacher pay the temple tax?"

When Jesus knew about the question, He told Peter, "Go to the lake and throw out your line. Take the first fish you catch; open its mouth and you will find a four-drachma coin. Take it and give it to them for my tax and yours" (Matthew 17:24, 27).

"God had provided our last $50,000," says Ralph, "out of the fish's mouth."

Many of the creditors who received their final payments, both then and earlier, were amazed at the Meloons' desire to repay. To them, it was a miracle akin to finding money inside a fish. They commended the Meloons for their Christian convictions and integrity.

"There are probably no people we can think of who would give consideration in such an honorable fashion," wrote one company president.

"It gives me a great faith in humanity to see someone like yourself step forth and pay an honestly incurred debt," another wrote. And one executive said, "I was flabbergasted to learn that someone remembered an obligation that goes back twenty-five years."

To the Meloons, however, it was simply a matter of honoring God and doing business according to His principles. They thanked Him that He had allowed them to be His witnesses in this way.

Notes

1. John S. Tompkins, "These Good Guys Finish First," *Reader's Digest,* June 1992, 142.

Chapter 6
The Turnaround

*A*s he speaks to audiences about Correct Craft's bankruptcy and how the business returned to life, repaying all its debts, Ralph Meloon likes to tell about the short conversation two little boys had while being chased by a dog: "One little boy said, 'I'm going to stop and pray.' The other said, 'I'm going to *run* and pray.'"

"During the time we were in bankruptcy proceedings," Ralph continues, "we were running and praying; we were driving and praying; we were doing a lot of things, always with prayer." Ralph's point is that financial troubles must be fought, that bankruptcy is not the first alternative. If it does come, however, creditors should be repaid, whether 10, 20, or 100 percent of what they're owed. Most who hear the story of Correct Craft's turnaround agree it's a dramatic example of faith in God.

Ralph and W. O. tell their story of vision and faith regularly to couples facing business bankruptcy. Since 1985, the two have been the chief speakers at Turnaround Weekends, a program of Turnaround Ministries. On average, nine times each year the Meloons and Turnaround's executive director, Van Thurston, lead the weekend meetings in conference centers near Atlanta, New York's Adirondacks, and Southern California.

This ministry, independent of Correct Craft (though the business does contribute to the nonprofit outreach), started after the Meloons' remarkable comeback led to requests for meetings. Years before the debt was totally paid off, Ralph and W. O. were telling the story to groups around the world. W. O. first told it publicly to missionaries on the south coast of Irian Jaya who needed $50,000 to replace a hospital that had washed into the sea. Repeating the thought that "God is not poor," W. O. inspired them to trust their Lord for the money. In the next two years, $100,000 came in.

The story of the Meloons' determination to fight bankruptcy and repay their debts appeared in three Christian magazines prior to their repaying the final creditor in 1984. Since then, it has appeared in three other Christian publications, including *Decision* magazine, as well as in *Reader's Digest* and a college textbook. (See the beginning of the next chapter.) A *Guideposts* article appeared in November 1973, after a New York couple, teetering on the verge of bankruptcy, contacted the Meloons. Ernie and Ruth Jones were new Christians and owners of a Correct Craft. For three days, the Meloons counseled and prayed with them. Later the couple contacted Richard H. Schneider, then senior editor of *Guideposts,* with the story of the Meloons' faith and encouragement.

Turnaround Ministries hosts forty people at each weekend, typically husbands and wives. Turnaround has a waiting list of more than 200 couples, and Thurston believes that during an economic downturn, the backlog will increase to several thousand. All expenses for the weekend—lodging, meals, and transportation (even airfare for those coming from out of state) —are paid by the ministry. Alumni and other supporters of Turnaround supply its budget.[1]

TWENTY-FIVE YEARS OF PREPARATION

Many people hear about the weekend from others who have attended. The Meloons' candor and compassion drive the weekend. "It's successful because God prepared us well—the preparation was twenty-five years," W. O. explains, referring to the time (1960–1984) the business endured bankruptcy.

At a Turnaround Weekend in early 1997 in Southern California's San Bernardino mountains, the Meloons were joined by their wives, their lawyer, Jim Welch, and two alumni couples from prior Turnarounds. Speaking before almost forty guests, the two couples told about their poor decisions that led to the bankruptcy. Both husbands said they ignored their wives' warnings and did not pray for God's guidance before making major financial decisions. Welch explained the role and limitations of a lawyer in a business bankruptcy. "Don't rely on your attorney for everything," he said. "Attorneys are human beings. . . . Stay in contact with your creditors. God used the Meloons and worked through them. He did it." The best advice, Welch said, will come from God.

Much of the human advice that weekend came from W. O. and Ralph Meloon. "Your state of affairs is not punishment," W. O. emphasized. "God is not punishing you. He's preparing you for the future." Many people have the mistaken belief that bankruptcy is God's judgment, he said, but a loving God wants them to grow close to Him. "I can remember some of my best friends at the church would say behind me, 'I wonder what Walt did that God has to treat him like this.' Even at our churches, this sort of thing happens."

Bankruptcy is like any difficult time, a chance to stretch and grow, the Meloons said. "We often pray for God to make things easy on us," W. O. told the couples. "But you won't learn a thing from something that comes easily. You will only learn when you're scrubbing it out and the skin's coming off your fingers. It's the hard things you profit from." And God will sustain and restore those who suffer loss, although not always to the same material success. When he does, said Ralph, "Be careful. We need to give the credit where the credit is due—to God."

The Meloons' strongest caution is to persevere with trust in a compassionate and powerful God. "It's always too soon to quit," the Meloons said throughout the weekend. "Don't refuse to quit just on the future, either, but also on your spouse and your God. God can help you deal with the disappointments and setbacks of financial loss and of pursuing creditors and tax agents," the Meloons added.

Lectures don't make up the entire weekend seminar, however. Husbands and wives spend time talking about their desires and fears. Though Thurston and the Meloons are available for perspective and to be listening ears, they usually don't offer advice or solutions for specific situations. When someone requests counsel, Thurston first encourages the person to discuss the business problems with his own spouse. Wives have keen insight into their husbands' strengths and weaknesses in running a business, according to Thurston.

At the end of one Turnaround Weekend, for instance, Thurston had talked a couple of times with a man whose business had floundered, and now he asked to talk with the wife. The woman began by praising her husband: "Well, I've got the most wonderful husband in the world. He's sweet, and he's kind and generous. He loves his children, and he loves me." Then she paused before continuing, "But he doesn't have any business running a business, because he doesn't know anything about it. If he could sell, he could make a fortune. But he cannot run a business."

Thurston notes, "I had just spent three days coming to that conclusion, and she already knew it." The wife had expressed that opinion earlier at home, Thurston adds, "but he didn't listen." After talking further with his wife and Thurston, the man decided to close the business. He soon became a salesman for one of his previous suppliers. The outcome, Thurston later learned, was dramatic: "In the first year, just selling—with no money problems to deal with—he made $100,000."

In most cases when Thurston counsels, he finds that the wife "knows the problem and the solution, because she lives with it every day."

Over the course of twenty-two years, Van Thurston owned more than twenty different businesses, as many as six at one time. Now he directs Turnaround Ministries and is president of Applied Business Concepts, the ministry that runs the Turnaround Weekends. Like W. O. and Ralph, he is convinced that, in most cases, the cause of financial problems that lead to near or actual bankruptcy is spiritual. "It requires a spiritual solution," he asserts.

In the closing session of the Turnaround Weekend, Van discusses the audience's spiritual needs. He tells them, "You have to make a commitment and say, 'This is it. I'm going to do what God says. I'm going to talk with Him, and I will be an example of what Jesus Christ would do if He were here now. If you're not willing to do that, you are just playing games. You can't do it in your own strength, and that's what you've been trying to do.

"It's going to be tough after you get home," he adds. "Remember, it's not your circumstances that are your problem —it's your relationship."

Relationships, especially with God but also with one's mate, form the focus of the weekend. The Meloons and Thurston come back to the theme that one must know and trust God during financial straits, that He is worthy of such trust. Financial principles are important and are discussed, but they're secondary to one's trust in a good heavenly Father. Most attendees are Christians, though some come without a Christian belief. They all hear a compelling story of the Meloons' faith.

"God sees the end from the beginning," W. O. declares. "The God who 'owns the cattle upon a thousand hills' could have orchestrated our solvency years ago, but we were not yet ready for it. There were too many things we still had to learn. . . . This business belongs to Him.

"Moses' forty years in the wilderness didn't mean a thing to me until we spent years wandering under the cloud of bankruptcy. It wasn't the shortest route, but God has His purposes." In retrospect, some of those purposes already seem clear.

Ralph says the bankruptcy changed his attitudes toward Scripture and money. "I spent much more time in the Word," he reports. "I spent much more time on my knees. And I certainly began to return much more money to the Lord. I just returned it, because I don't own it anyway. Before, we were happy to give 15 percent. Even Uncle Sam knows we ought to do better than that. The IRS allows us 50 percent. People can give 50 percent and take it off their income tax. That means Uncle Sam is paying 35 percent of it [through tax deductions]."

Even during the bankruptcy, the Meloons did not stop tithing; they still gave 10 percent of their limited income. They cut their pay to $100 a week while paying their truck drivers twice as much. "We had to make this business go somehow," W. O. says. Although they each gave a tithe, W. O. tells those who ask that he is not an "avid tither." The tithe suggests that God owns only 10 percent, and "I don't think you can count one dollar that God does not own," W. O. says. Today they don't practice tithing at all, giving much more than 10 percent of their income. "Now we understand tithing was under the Law," Ralph says, "and we are stewards of *all* God has entrusted to us."

SAYING "THANK YOU" BY GIVING

As they repaid their creditors, the thankful Meloons began donating their moneys in larger proportions. Since 1984, Walt and Ralph have given at least 50 percent of their income to charities and missions. The company itself gave 10 percent in corporate donations, the maximum tax deduction allowed by law. When the company had strong profits, the Meloons received bonuses; they in turn gave their entire bonuses to missionaries and mission agencies.

"Ever since we learned our lesson [from the bankruptcy] and have been blessed, we give," W. O. says. He regularly tells Turnaround Weekend guests, "You can't outgive God. He owns the cattle on a thousand hills. His resources are unlimited. What God wants is not our money, but you and me totally dedicated."

A few times they have given more than 50 percent. In 1996, the IRS "took a long look," as W. O. puts it, at the

Meloons' records, and that wasn't the first time. The tax agents could not believe these men in their late seventies and early eighties (W. O. turned eighty-one in 1996) were giving away their money so readily.

"They wanted to know if we found a way to get extra money into our own pockets—or the pockets of some family members," W. O. says. But the Meloons' accountant had all their records. By looking at the receipts and talking to Meloon business contacts, the agents soon learned that W. O. and Ralph are men with big hearts and great faith.

A ZEAL FOR OTHERS

As their colleague in Turnaround Ministries, Thurston observes two businessmen who are consistent in their zeal for others. He is impressed that W. O. sometimes understates his role in bringing the company back, and he finds the humility extends to how W. O. puts others first. Until mediocre health forced him to fly first class, the elder executive flew coach regularly. "He will go to the back seat constantly," Thurston says. "He's a living example of humility."

Ralph's heart for the spiritually lost also impresses Van, who remembers meeting Ralph at Atlanta's Hartsfield Airport for one Turnaround Weekend being held in suburban Atlanta. Van explained he had to meet other Turnaround guests at the baggage claim, so Ralph went with him. Later, after a gentleman spotted the Turnaround sign in Van's hands and they turned to locate his luggage, Van looked around and could no longer see Ralph. As the man went for his luggage, Van began searching for Ralph.

He soon found Ralph helping someone with his baggage. "He had helped him carry it to the chairs," Van says. "He sat there talking with him. Then he had started to do it again with someone else."

Van later learned from Ralph the nature of the conversation. "He was saying, 'Oh, let me help you with your bags. Where are you coming from?'

"'Chicago.'

"'Would you like to know where you're going? Let me help you over here with your bags, and let me tell you how you can be assured of where you'll be for eternity.' My! He never misses the opportunity to talk about Christ," Van marvels. "He was on the other side of the room, 'working the crowd.'"

In the retreat setting, guests listen closely to the Meloons' story. W. O. believes that "a big part of where they're getting their blessing is realizing, 'Here's the man that this happened to. He's been through it, and God got him out.' They just need the example there to encourage them."

One New York businessman, a gifted public speaker and an officer in the Toastmasters Club, heard the Meloons and found himself crying for the first time in four years of legal battles to save his business. Later he wrote W. O. to explain his response: "For the first time in over four years, I was with people who cared. With the help of all the tears and hugs this weekend, I'm ready for some productive time. This time, with God's help and guidance it will be a work effort that will last."

The New York executive had led a business buyout in the early 1980s, making millions of dollars, and had business leaders visiting him to learn his technique. Once termed "nearly invincible" by a national magazine, he later lost a $63 million project that cost him millions in personal cash. Eventually, as he went through the courts, he would lose everything, including his home. "My pride stole from my family," he wrote W. O. But because of the weekend, "my head is starting to clear and . . . I'm ready for some productive time."

LEARNING TO TRUST

Not all guests at the Turnaround retreat weekends are high-powered executives, but all are hard-working people, just like the Meloons. And like the Meloons, they wrestle with relationship issues with people and God, especially issues of trust and forgiveness.

A Georgia construction company owner and his wife had

just walked through both corporate and personal bankruptcy. "God's grace is sufficient," they conclude.

An Indiana couple face bankruptcy, forced by a bank that closed its doors and by the suicide of the prime financial offender. "One of our greatest needs," the couple admits, "is to be willing and able to forgive those who were unfair—those responsible for our financial difficulty."

A Texan with a reputation as a good manager, never before in financial difficulty, says how good it is to be among people who really care. "I have people I owe money to, and I really want to pay them, but I can't," he reports.

A Nebraskan, who came close to bankruptcy four years previously, tells others at the retreat, "Don't let poverty or self-sufficiency rob you of the joy of the miraculous. And in recovery, don't forget to thank God."

These people return home to face the future with new hope and perspective. The problems are still there, but somehow they now seem less formidable. Some still move into bankruptcy, yet they learn to trust and thank God for His goodness. Others recover from their financial difficulties, seeing God at work in direct ways.

One owner of a failed highway construction company attended a Turnaround with his wife after heavy debts forced him to file personal bankruptcy. Nick and Ellen (not their real names) lost their home shortly after returning from the retreat. Nick went to work at his brother-in-law's construction business. He owed his sister and brother-in-law several hundred thousand dollars from the failure of his Florida business. Within the year, his relative's business was awarded two contracts valued at almost $7 million, and Nick received a large year-end bonus. Three months later, the two projects were completed, and Nick's brother-in-law returned the original notes marked "paid in full" for Nick's work at the highly successful business.

"The success of our projects which allowed this debt repayment is probably a once-in-a-lifetime success from a contractor perspective," Nick wrote W. O. "It is beyond explanation.

However, I think I like it that way. Because if this could be explained, perhaps I would . . . take some of the credit. But this turnaround is so far beyond my comprehension that I can only stand humbly and say my Lord and Savior Jesus Christ has performed a miracle. He gets all the credit, and through my human reasoning I cannot take any of it."

W. O. reminds attendees that not all bankruptcy is financial, and that everyone must beware of another kind of bankruptcy. Total loss has been around since the Fall in the Garden of Eden. "There was bankruptcy with Adam and Eve, not in dollars and cents, but total bankruptcy of discipline to do God's will when Cain killed Abel," he tells them. "David repeatedly faced bankruptcy. When Moses killed the Egyptian, he had to run for the desert. All of their experiences had the same elements found in financial bankruptcy.

"Divorce is nothing but a bankruptcy of love and affection," he adds. "I believe God wants to handle all bankruptcy in the same way." People must always come to God humbly, recognizing their own mistakes and depending on Him alone for restoration. That's when the real turnaround begins.

Note

1. Van Thurston estimates that a Turnaround Weekend costs between $12,000 and $15,000. The Fellowship of Christian Companies, International (FCCI), encouraged the Meloons to begin the ministry, and FCCI continues to refer businesspeople to Turnaround. (One Turnaround Weekend also meets each year near Tyler, Texas.) For more information, contact Turnaround Ministries, P. O. Box 760, Gainesville, GA 30503; 770-503-9038.

   Thurston has written a helpful book dealing with recovery from bankruptcy entitled *Hope at the Bottom* (Chicago: Moody, 1996).

Chapter 7
A Principled Company

*E*ach year, business students at more than 130 colleges and universities read about the Meloons' principled stand against a corrupt government inspector. Correct Craft is the major case study introducing "Ethics in the Business System," a chapter in the textbook *Business, Government, and Society.* The company's refusal to pay off the inspector and its insistence on paying back 100 percent of what it owed its creditors—even to the point of searching for them—has marked it as a standard-bearer for ethical values in the marketplace.

"Correct Craft is a company which is driven by ethical values," wrote George Steiner, the book's coauthor. "These values, derived from the philosophy and example of its founder, permeate the company culture to direct employees and influence strategic decisions." Steiner, emeritus professor of management at UCLA, concluded, "[Correct Craft's] story illustrates how ethical values can have a continuous impact on the fortunes of a business."[1]

Reader's Digest spotlighted Correct Craft as a company that follows the Golden Rule in treating customers and vendors well. In "These Good Guys Finish First," John S. Tompkins recounted the bankruptcy and repayment of debtors and quoted

Walt N. Meloon summarizing the firm's business success: "It all comes down to treating others as you want to be treated."[2]

The chief executive of Levi Strauss, another company featured in the *Reader's Digest* profile, explained that clothier's —and indirectly the boatbuilder's—success:

> A company's values are crucial to its competitive success. You can't be one thing and say another. People can detect fakes unerringly. They won't put values into practice if you're not practicing them.[3]

Correct Craft continues to practice its ethical values today. Indeed, W. N. Meloon's statement in the early 1990s—"I don't want to change just for the sake of money"—echoes that of his grandfather, W. C., almost sixty years earlier: "If you have made a decision based only on money, you have made a bad decision." The Correct Craft management remains committed to its founding values.

For instance, Vice President of Marketing Larry Meddock once withdrew advertising from two major water-ski magazines because of questionable content. Though it meant no marketing presence in the national magazines, Correct Craft management defended its action to the board of directors.

One magazine featured lots of scantily clad models to illustrate its stories. Many dealers and some customers criticized the company for not running the ads; they couldn't understand the decision. The second magazine conducted boat tests in an allegedly unfair and misleading manner. Correct Craft withdrew its ads when the results were printed.

"What should we do?" Meddock asked the directors when they questioned the decision to pull the ad from the magazine that published the test results. "Should we say, 'It's okay that you participate in programs that are deceiving the public?'

"What do you want us to do?" Meddock again asked the directors. "It makes my life easier to be in those magazines. But what's our stand? I think Correct Craft is a principled company.

We have principles, and it's difficult to stand by them at times. But we must."

The directors agreed. They appreciated the stand by Meddock and President W. N. Meloon, and they applauded the decision to stick to beliefs that once again influenced a business outcome. And Meddock, ever the keen marketer, realized he had stumbled onto a new marketing campaign. Within a year, he and his staff had developed a new marketing program focusing on "a principled company." They created four ads to run for six months in several leading trade magazines. Each looked at one aspect of their Nautique line of ski boats and how it demonstrated the firm principles that guide the boatbuilder.

"Nautiques are built on a solid foundation of principles," each ad began. The four principles highlighted were (1) customer satisfaction; (2) quality in construction, warranty, and "driveability"; (3) safety, as measured by being the only inboard boatbuilder to receive a "preferred builder" rating by a major marine insurer; and (4) maintaining the lowest water wake and spray in the industry. The first ad touted a phenomenal approval rating from its customers: "Correct Craft has 97% customer satisfaction. That's as good as Mercedes, Lexus, and BMW, and outranks all inboard ski boats, too!" The ad's final line, like the other three ads, read, "When it's time to buy . . . base it on principle." (See chapter 11 for more on customer response to the company.)

The principled company demonstrates its values in many ways. But three of the most telling are in advertising, corporate sponsorship, and honesty.

THE RIGHT PHOTOS, THE RIGHT MESSAGE

Correct Craft carefully monitors the content of its ads, particularly the photographs used. In an industry where some competitors promote their products with strong sex appeal, using attractive women in skimpy bikinis, Correct Craft makes sure the women in its ads will not make Sunday school teachers blush. The same wholesome policy affects the pictorial content of its annual catalogs and product brochures.

"If I were sitting in a Sunday school class with others or in the church pew and I'd be uncomfortable looking at this woman in this bathing suit, we don't want it in our literature," says W. N. Meloon. "If I can't take my brochure into the church and lay it on the pew and feel comfortable about one of the little old ladies coming in and looking at it, I've got no business printing it."

A few photo shoots for ads have produced pictures that were inappropriate, and Meloon understands one major reason. Some women boaters simply wear smaller swimsuits now than in years past. He points out, though, that in slalom skiing, most women wear one-piece swimsuits, and in jump skiing most don fuller bodysuits.

The Meloons use one overriding criterion in business decisions, whether about photos of women or changing vendors who supply parts for their boats: The decision must be consistent with deeply held Christian principles. "If I can't make the same decision in this office at 9 o'clock on Monday morning that I would make sitting in church at 9 o'clock on Sunday morning, I have no business making that decision," W. N. asserts.

SAYING NO TO ALCOHOL SPONSORS

Correct Craft has helped to sponsor dozens of water-ski tournaments since the 1960s. In fact, it has been the official towboat of the world championships throughout the 1990s, pulling professional skiers at the Worlds in Singapore ('93), France ('95), and Colombia('97); it has the inside track for landing the 1999 world tournament in Italy as well. Correct Craft also has been the exclusive towboat of the U. S. Masters since 1973 and co-towboat (with two others) of the U. S. Open during the '90s.

In a sport where being named "the official towboat" brings recognition as being a premier ski boat maker, Correct

Craft appreciates its selection. And with its Sport Nautique, it has won similar honors at most of the world wakeboarding tournaments in the 1990s, including the 1990 inaugural competition in Kauai.

Its closest competitors would love to sponsor these events. Yet one time Correct Craft turned down a chance to sponsor a major series of tournaments; in another instance, it surrendered valuable free publicity as a cosponsor. It took those actions because of its Christian principles: The company does not want its name and image associated with alcohol or tobacco products.

A few years ago, the company was invited to be a contributing sponsor of a series of pro ski tournaments that would be featured on ESPN. The eight competitions were being pulled by a major ski boat rival, and Correct Craft had a chance to replace the other company. The promotional value of being seen not only on this pro tour but also on ESPN was great. The offer was tempting. Yet the major sponsor was a big alcohol company. Correct Craft had a major decision to make.

"Our competitor had it, and a lot of people said to us, 'Why don't you do it? You'd be bigger than they are. They're bigger than you are,'" W. N. recalls. (The big three inboard ski boat manufacturers, Correct Craft, MasterCraft, and Malibu, have rotated among the top three positions during the 1990s.) "We had a chance to take over the tour as a sponsor. In other words, 'Buy the position and do it.'"

But did the company want to be affiliated with the alcohol company that was the main sponsor? That's the question the president asked himself, and soon he was asking it of business friends and advisers. He knew the position of his father and uncle, the two previous presidents. They opposed any association. But he wondered if such separation was still realistic. A major conflict arose within himself, and he sought further counsel. He asked a couple of board members who had wrestled with it in their own businesses. He asked two men who were general managers of National Basketball Association teams. Both told him it was a necessary compromise in an imperfect world, as they worked for others who owned the teams. One noted that he did not serve alcoholic beverages at any team receptions he organized.

W. N. called several others, including his personal mentor, Harry Conn. Then he retreated to the family's small vacation home in Speculator, New York, to relax, pray, and sort through the issues. The night before he returned to Florida, he had an unusual dream. He found himself surrounded by boats stacked up to his head, so many he couldn't see anything else. Suddenly, "the boats were gone, and I was giving this guy this boat, he was giving me the money, and I continued to sell him boats. There was nothing but this huge pile of money. And while I was dealing with the money, I was asking myself how much of that is mine."

W. N. then awoke, confused by the scene. But he remembered that no one else was in the dream; he did all the work of gathering, selling, and delivering the boats. He took all the money. Now he wondered, *How much of that is mine?* "And then it dawned on me that none of it was mine. It belonged to the company stockholders. And God tells us that we obey the laws of man." That meant recognizing the will of the majority stockholders. And two stockholders who together had held a majority of shares longer than anyone were W. O. and Ralph Meloon, his father and uncle. Though W. N. is now CEO and president, he believes his two predecessors hold a special place in his life as relatives. "Scripture also tells me they're my elders. Respect them."

W. N. points out that he doesn't believe God normally gives visions. "I don't believe in dreams or visions or voices. . . . But this one time, as I was driving home to Florida with my wife, it began to dawn on me that I was talking and listening and handling this the wrong way. It came to the point that I wasn't in control; they were." And though, as a major stockholder himself and the company president, W. N. had input and deserved respect from the past presidents, he realized that "they were my elders. I should be listening to them." When he returned to his office, "I just picked up the phone and called and said, 'Hey, I want out of this thing.'"

The issue was settled. The prohibition against promoting alcohol remained, in this case by avoiding a strong affiliation with a major maker of alcoholic beverages.

The other issue in being wary of a cosponsorship with an alcohol company, W. N. says, is that "Scripture does tell us we should refrain from the appearance of evil." But the main factor in rejecting the offer was his respect for his elders. He would honor their wishes and the company's tradition.

The policy has been modified only slightly since that incident. Beer companies remain a major sponsor of most pro water-ski competitions, and any boat manufacturer wishing to become the official towboat faces the prospect of finding a beer sponsor with its signs at the tournaments. If Correct Craft were to boycott all tournaments with any alcohol sponsors, it would no longer be involved in many tournaments. So it draws the line that it will not participate as an official sponsor when an alcohol company is the major sponsor, nor will it allow its signs to appear near those of a beer company.

"We ask that we be listed only as the official towboat of the event," W. N. says. "Even if we give a lot of money, we don't want the name 'sponsor' put on us. It ties us too close. We're not comfortable."

W. N. goes on to explain, "We are to be in the world, not of the world," paraphrasing John 17:16. "Part of my world includes such sponsors, but we don't have to be that close to them."

Recently, when the world wakeboard championships were held in Altamonte Springs, Florida, the company had another decision to make. The main sponsor again was an alcohol company, and Correct Craft had been the official towboat at most previous world championships. The solution was to continue as sponsor but adopt a more low-profile position. The company sacrificed valuable publicity in order not to ally itself with the main sponsor.

"We backed out of the sponsorship position," W. N.

explains, "and said, 'Gentlemen, we will only be called the official towboat of the tournament, regardless of whether we paid
as much as the other company. We don't want to be identified in
the same level or in relationship to this beer company.' We went
to the tournament site, sent our people there, and moved our
signs so that [the beer company] and Correct Craft weren't side
by side or above or over each other.

"And the people who put on the tournament respected
our decision to take a lesser position because of principle. In
some cases, the publicity was not as much as we deserved,
because we just didn't want that close association."

"We said, 'Let's not have our signs next to theirs,'" adds
Scott Mohr, field marketing and promotions manager. "When
the premier sponsor is an alcohol company, we don't want to
have our name associated with theirs." He also offers an additional reason, a message Correct Craft wants to get to the
public: "We like to distance ourselves from the alcohol companies because we feel athletics and alcohol don't mix."

HONESTY AND INTEGRITY

Mike Elrod, a Correct Craft employee for more than twenty years and now vice president of production, says he stays
because of the company's integrity and honesty. "I work for
Correct Craft because of the Meloons' values and morals," he
states. "I've seen them do things that I daresay possibly no
other business would have done from a business sense. But
they thought it was the right thing to do. I personally think that's
the reason for their success. And that's why I like to work here.

"The company never asks you to do anything that's illegal
or borderline legal to make a profit." Elrod adds that the unwavering devotion to honesty has made it easy to spurn other job
offers: "I cannot put a dollar value on that honesty. From time
to time, I'm approached by a headhunter. It makes the ego feel
good that day, but you have to feel good at the end of the day,
too. These people are exceptional people."

Such honesty even compels the current and past presidents of the company to accept some blame for the bankruptcy. W. O. doesn't want to paint the Corps of Engineers and the corrupt inspector as pure villains, conspirators seeking to put the company out of business. Instead, he calls the boat-rejection episode "the final straw" that sank Correct Craft into bankruptcy. There were other reasons for the sinking, too, as they confessed during their ride to bankruptcy court (see page 63). The humble Meloons were willing to evaluate and learn from their own mistakes.

The key error, as W. O. noted, was selling stock to raise money for expansion. Not only was this raising new capital for the wrong reason—"to be big"—but it also allowed non-Christians to have a role in running the business. That violates a business principle to "not be unequally yoked" with nonbelievers in decision making, says W. O.

In the early 1950s, the business analysis firm Dunn and Bradstreet reported that Correct Craft was the country's second-largest builder of pleasure boats. That motivated the company to raise more capital through the stock offering. According to W. O., "If we were the second-largest builder, we wanted to be the first. And that's the wrong reason."

Management sold stock for several years. The stock never sold in large amounts, and the Meloons owned most of it, yet they attribute part of the bankruptcy pressures to going public without seeking direction from God. W. O. believes that during the subsequent bankruptcy, "the Lord was trying to tell us something: 'Boys, you're making a big mistake.'"

The mistake, says W. O., was "wanting to be big, doing it on our own. We began to tell the Lord what to do. Well, the Lord didn't furnish the money. So we looked to bankers, which was a mistake. We talked to accountants and attorneys, which was a mistake. They all said, 'If Dunn and Bradstreet says that about you and they've got the figures, you should put stock on the market and become the *biggest* company.'"

If you're number two in a business and you want to be number one, what's wrong with that? Nothing, unless the motive is wrong and the decision is made without asking God, the Meloons will tell you.

"We were telling God, 'We've got our own ideas; now You bless them.' You can't tell God that any louder than to make the moves—and we had started moving.

"God wanted us to know, 'Don't do it; you cannot become unequally yoked with unbelievers,'" W. O. adds, referring to 2 Corinthians 6:14. "The minute you have unbelievers with your stock, you're in violation of God's command. It took us a long time to realize that."

A second mistake, according to his son, W. N., was that Correct Craft continued to operate two plants. The company was slightly undercapitalized, and the Titusville plant, located fifty miles from the main factory, was draining resources. Consolidation was in order. But that would happen only after bankruptcy.

"The business was underfinanced," W. O. agrees. "If we had been adequately financed, we would have had two management teams to keep costs down." Correct Craft had extra expenses every time it moved inventories from Titusville to Orlando. Some days it had three trucks transferring inventory one hundred miles round-trip.

But the action by the inspector worsened the problems, W. O. acknowledges. The Corps of Engineers did not cancel the contract; it merely continued to reject the scores of boats coming off the production line. Had the Corps canceled the contract, the U. S. government would have had to pay all of Correct Craft's start-up costs, as well as a reasonable profit. W. O. believes that because of the end of World War II, the Corps and the corrupt inspector "had come to the place where they simply didn't want the boats."

Still, the rejected boats were only one element of the company's move toward bankruptcy.

"God had to sweep us clean," W. O. says of the management's mistakes. "Sweeping clean" meant the company went almost $1 million in debt. But God also turned the company around as it honored Him by rebuilding without seeking more shareholders and by repaying its creditors 100 percent, even though it wasn't required to do so.

"We never dreamed we could get from having $1 million less than zero to where we are today," W. O. says—one of America's premier ski boat builders.

Notes

1. George A. Steiner and John F. Steiner, *Business, Government, and Society,* 8th ed. (New York: McGraw-Hill, 1997), 180.
2. John S. Tompkins, "These Good Guys Finish First," *Reader's Digest,* June 1992, 141.
3. Ibid., 143.

Chapter 8
Treat Them Right

*C*hris Hadley enjoys building boats. As a department lead in deck webbing, she sprays fiberglass threads mixed with epoxy resin onto the boat deck and then brushes the mix evenly on the deck material; she also watches that those under her properly apply the materials. When she joined Correct Craft eleven years ago, she found the boatbuilding process "amazing." And today she says, "I'm still learning. We have had a new gun for the past two years. There are special techniques and troubleshooting to know." And her opinion matters. "When they make style changes, they let us give our opinion and suggestions."

Developing skill and having her ideas welcomed are just two of the reasons Hadley likes working at Correct Craft. As a teacher's aide who moonlights in a boat factory, Chris remembers that her boss, Mike Elrod, once showed her a newspaper story during a break: "It was about schools and a principal planning to turn a school around. He wanted my opinion. It's rare to find supervisors who talk about things besides work. He cares. Same with the main office: nice people to work for."

Among the employee benefits she enjoys are the company's matching pension plan and occasional free tickets to Orlando Magic basketball games and Solar Bear hockey games.

She also likes the availability of books and audio tapes through the company library. "They help you with problems," says the mother of two grown children who wants to keep her marriage strong.

Vicky Greco, upholstery foreman on the day shift, also appreciates the working environment. "They are good to their people," she says. "I learned how to design an interior, and my supervisor wanted my opinion." Vicky says she likes to work with her hands, and she has helped add the interiors to Ski Nautiques for five years. She supervises fifteen workers, setting schedules and making sure fabrics are in as they should be. The upholstery crew installs vinyl covers on side panels (called the combing) on the front driver's and passenger seats and the engine cover, as well as covering the speaker grills with fabric.

Many of her seamstresses work upstairs, where the factory heat rises and the Florida sun bakes the roof above. The sewing crew was delighted a couple of years ago when the company installed air conditioning for that one department. (Those on the main floor settle for the daily breezes that usually blow through the large factory doors.)

Like Chris, Vicky enjoys watching professional sports and loves receiving complimentary tickets to at least one Magic basketball game each year. Now that her oldest son is in college, she usually treats her husband and teenage son to a free game, and sometimes she goes with her husband.

KEEPING EMPLOYEES HEALTHY AND WISE

Correct Craft management has always believed it must treat right those who make the company a success: customers, dealers, vendors, and certainly employees. The more than 120 workers at the factory and scores more in research, development, marketing, and administration benefit from a clear corporate policy of honoring employees. As W. N. once said, "Correct Craft also has a commitment to its employees, helping each develop to his full potential in skill, knowledge, creativity, technical know-how, job satisfaction, and quality of life."[1]

The company provides free dental insurance and a free $25,000 life insurance policy for each worker. In 1996, the company paid 84 percent of total health and dental insurance for its employees and 64 percent for their dependents. Employees working three years can buy a Correct Craft boat at a substantial discount. The company also offers a continuing education program and operates an employee loan program to help workers with short-term emergencies.

An employee can apply for educational assistance with any goal, whether completing a high school education or post-graduate work. The only requirements are that the employee state his educational goal, that it benefits the company, and that the employee maintains passing grades while enrolled. One year, for instance, an employee in accounting with a master's degree took additional courses part-time with Correct Craft support.

The education program is "available to anyone who wants continuing education and needs financial help," says W. N. "Someone may want to go back and need some assistance in getting their high school equivalency. We'll work with them in that area." If the request is for significantly "more than we have done for others," the management group will discuss the request, the president says. "We'll talk about it, and we'll decide what we can do to help. Some will come and say, 'Any help I can get is going to be great' or 'I need the full amount.' We have to take a look at it."

Employee health also means keeping workers cool in the Florida sun. The limited air conditioning at the factory makes some summer days very warm. To help, the morning shift begins at 5:30 and breaks as the afternoon sun starts to bear down. The second shift arrives in midafternoon, "so no one gets the full heat of the day," W. N. says. And the plant intentionally closes the final two weeks of July for equipment maintenance and retooling for the upcoming model year, while all plant workers take two weeks of vacation.

"We try to do what we can to make it more comfortable,"

W. N. explains. "This industry is labor intensive. And being in
Florida, labor intensive in the summer is not a good time. We
schedule our plant shutdown to hit in the middle of the hottest
part of the weather and kind of break it. We do that to help the
employees."

Clearly, the factory workers appreciate the treatment. The
cost of labor, a key measure of worker productivity, averages
5.3 percent at Correct Craft, compared with an average of 11
percent in the boating industry. Many factors contribute to
keeping costs low, but certain company policies help, including
merit pay (salary increases based solely on performance), versatile workers (they learn several tasks to help others), and
supervisors who lead by example.

At times, impressed vendors have noticed the busy plant
personnel. "Are these people always working this hard?" some
vendors have asked manufacturing supervisors. One vendor
told production vice president Mike Elrod that he had just
come from another efficient plant "where the workers were
very productive, and they walked from one job to another. Your
people tend to run."

"I don't advocate running," Elrod notes. "That's not good
for safety, but our people do work very hard. They look at the
examples of the supervisors and feel they're not being singled
out. They're willing to participate. They work hard, and at the
end of the day they feel good."

Elrod, like the rest of the management team, values his
employees. Speaking in his second-floor office that overlooks
the factory below, he says, "We have some valuable and sensitive equipment out there. But none of it is as sensitive as the
people walking through that plant every day. At the very least,
you may have equipment that's broken; you may not know
what's the matter with it. But when people come through that
gate, you don't know what's been happening. Have they been up
all night with a sick child, or do they have a kid on drugs?

"I treat everybody like I'd want to be treated. I don't think
I'm better than anybody out there. . . . I'd like to think I lead by

example. I put in my time with the shifts." One week, for instance, he came to the plant three nights at 11 P.M. to observe and help a busy crew.

Each employee also receives a company thank-you on his or her birthday—a personal holiday and a birthday card with "a small amount of cash to go out and have supper with their spouse," says W. N.

As a family-owned business, Correct Craft does not object if several members of the same family work at the company, though they won't be in the same department. At present, at least three families have either brothers and sisters or father-daughter or father-son combinations on the payroll. W. N. remembers once having four members of a family working there. "That's a little unusual," he says. "Vernon Riddle worked in the machine shop, his wife worked in the mail room, his son worked on the production line, and his daughter worked in transportation. His children, Rick and Sherry, are still here."

It speaks well of the company that one family member invites another to apply for employment at his workplace. "It's pleasing to know they are so loyal. We do hire family, though we don't make it a priority," W. N. notes. When a second family member is hired, management makes it clear there will be no favoritism.

"It's only fair," W. N. explains. "If they expect that because one of them has a job the other is going to keep his job, that's not right. It's not fair to the other employees, it's not fair to the company, and it's not fair to the individual. So we bring the rest of the family in and say, 'It's great that you all want to be here, but everybody is going to do their ninety-day probation just like everybody else. And on the eighty-ninth day, if there's a disagreement, it's all over.'"

As a third-generation Correct Craft employee himself, W. N. can appreciate some of the challenges of family members working at the same place. (He discusses the challenge of leading a family-run business in the next chapter.)

Layoffs and *downsizing* are two words that have made

workers everywhere cringe in the 1990s. When it comes to cost cutting and improving the bottom line, employees are often seen as expendable. But that's not the attitude at Correct Craft, which has laid off staff only twice in its history. The most recent time was in 1995, when the company closed its boat trailer division to concentrate exclusively on boats. Whether the employees there had worked two years or more than twenty, *all* were offered jobs elsewhere in the company. Rather than fire them and then later rehire new workers to fill openings in boat manufacturing, the company absorbed the trailer division workers, fitting some into positions similar to their old jobs and retraining others.

Of about thirteen people in the division, only a couple chose to leave. Five remained at the converted welding shop, where they now prepare aluminum parts used in the boats. One who chose to be retrained for a new job was a painter who learned to gelcoat boats. "It's spray painting, but it's still different," says production vice president Elrod, who had supervised the trailer division. He appreciates the compassion shown to his workers, as well as the wise use of a skilled, existing workforce.

"Once again, at a lot of businesses, because some of the people had been there many years and had higher hourly wages, the decision would have been just to lay them off," Elrod says. "That was not what we did."

Thirty-five years earlier, the company had its only major layoff when bankruptcy caused it to cut most of its workforce, dropping from 225 workers to only 25. The company honored those with seniority and proven loyalty. "They laid off the most recent hires but kept the older men," recalls J. T. Jones, who stayed in hardware and trim. J. T. retired after working forty years with the company, and he explained why he spent most of his career at Correct Craft.

"I knew they were honest people," he says, "and they would do what they said. They always tried to take care of you. When we did a good job, like meeting an important deadline, they'd give a free lunch and bonuses to the men. You had your ups and downs—you have that on any job—but they were fair."

KEEPING THE CUSTOMERS SATISFIED

The company also wants to show fairness to its customers. Warranties are important to them, and most Correct Craft boat owners regard the company's policy as fair. The lifetime warranty includes defects in materials and workmanship and the structural integrity of the boat. The decision to offer a lifetime warranty came after the company tired of the game of one-upmanship with its competitors and realized it had often been granting warranty extensions anyway for the sake of keeping customers satisfied.

"Our competitors were giving six months, and we were giving three months," says W. N. "Then they were doing a year and we were doing six months. Then they were doing five years and we were doing a year.

"We said, 'This doesn't make a lot of sense. We're doing this because of them. Why don't we have a warranty based on what *we* do?' When we went back and did some research, we found we were basically warrantying some of this stuff, with policy adjustments and after-warranty adjustments, for years.

"Sometimes we would explain to a customer, 'Look, this boat is out of warranty. And you're the third owner. But because this is a Correct Craft, we're willing to work with you on this. Do you feel this would be acceptable?'" Sometimes Correct Craft would divide repair costs in thirds: the company paid one-third, the dealer paid one-third, and the individual paid the final third. Other times, a disgruntled customer would call headquarters complaining of having to pay for a mechanical problem he thought should be covered by warranty. The customer may have violated a small aspect of the warranty but would complain that shouldn't invalidate it. To satisfy the customer, the dealer and headquarters agreed to pay half the cost of repair if the customer paid the other half. In fact, internal research showed the company had always extended help to dissatisfied owners, even when the warranty had expired.

As W. N. explains, "Being a Correct Craft boat, it's just like having my name written on the side of the boat."

So management decided to offer a lifetime warranty in 1991, one of the first in the industry. Today a lifetime warranty is offered by about half the inboard-boat companies. The Correct Craft warranty is fully transferable should the boat be sold.

According to W. N., the move toward the lifetime warranty was assured when the company was able to answer yes to two questions: (1) Are we building a product that can stand up to the demands of a lifetime warranty? (2) Are we willing to face the costs? To answer the second question, they studied the historic costs of warranty work.

"It's a big decision," W. N. says. "When you're a Christian and you put something in writing and say something, you'd better be ready to back it up."

The company believes it offers a true lifetime warranty. W. N. says that with some companies, proving a defect under a lifetime warranty may cost more in legal fees than the warranty is worth. "'Lifetime warranty' is almost like smoke and mirrors with those firms," he says. "As a boat owner, it makes you feel real good, but try to collect on it. After twenty years, how are you going to prove a defect was caused by the boat's workmanship or materials? A guy may collect, but only after he spent some time and money for attorneys and other things."

Today, most builders offering lifetime warranties include a clause that makes disagreements between customer and seller subject to review by a board of arbitration. "But we do need to keep the customer happy," W. N. says. In fact, as a Christian company, Correct Craft tries not only to please customers but also to maintain a witness of integrity and a reputation for going the extra mile to help them.

"When it becomes a question of your character and your testimony, it's pretty simple," W. N. explains. "You just ask the customer, 'Look, what's going to make you happy?' Or you may say to him, 'All right, we'll take your boat back, you give us $4,000, and we'll put you in a brand-new boat, because your boat is three years old or four years old, and you did use it for that period of time.' That's justifiable.

"He may come back and say, 'No, I'm not giving you $4,000; I'll give you $2,000.' Well, now we aren't arguing about what we are as a company but about the price, and there's no need to do that.

"It gets real tricky when you're really a Christian in business. If they ask for your coat, you give them your coat. . . . If the Bible is the book we live by, we've got to live by it from the front page to the back. I wish I always did that. I don't. But God does allow me at times the patience, the virtue, and the wisdom to do that, and I can practice it."

W. N. remembers one customer who owned a Nautique three years and had three or four problems during that period. All were handled to his satisfaction, under warranty and in some cases going beyond the warranty. But when Jack (not his real name) planned to host a party aboard the boat and the craft had another breakdown, he'd had enough. He finally called the head office and got through to the president.

"This is a piece of junk," he said. "You've treated me poorly. I didn't think that Christians would do—"

"Whoa!" W. N. replied. He had heard enough. He was ready to answer for the name of the company and the validity of his faith. "Sir, now that you've brought it to this level of what I and this company are supposed to do or how I'm supposed to make a decision as a Christian, you tell me what I should do as a Christian."

The outcome of such a conversation may cost money, Meloon says, but "I don't think you can afford to let there be any question. . . . It's God's business, not mine.

"True, God can take adversity and turn it around. He can take that bad situation and make it good. But more important, you may have a man who is not a Christian, who doesn't understand. And for a boat you're going to let him go to hell? I don't think so. Not for a boat or the name Correct Craft or what he thought we should have done."

In that case and similar ones, the company negotiated a solution that met the customer's needs. That solution can range from fixing the problem, to giving a credit, to supplying a new boat or a similar used boat.

"There are various situations available; we try to approach each one so that it's a win-win outcome," W. N. says. Most important, though, are people. "If we say, 'Everything done for man won't last, but everything that's done for God does last,' then I'd better not be trying to please man under his rules, which say, 'You can't do that because that costs the company money.'" To let profits rule the decision, W. N. concludes, would show "a total disregard for the witness of this family and this company."

Besides, friendly—even extraordinary—customer service makes good business sense. "A happy customer tells about four people of his experience," W. N. concludes. "An unhappy customer tells about twenty people. So we do our best to keep a customer happy."

HELPING THE DEALERS

Each August, dozens of dealers gather in Orlando for three days to learn about the features and selling points of Correct Craft's new models. Congratulations and recognition are given for good sales performances; incentives to keep up the good work are offered; and the dealers encourage each other frequently. The nice setting in a first-class hotel is another reward, and many dealers bring their wives and families.

Like the company management, many of the dealers who sell Ski Nautiques are Christians. All are business and sales people who recognize a good product. Many are water-ski enthusiasts as well. Tim Sherwin, Correct Craft's largest dealer in total sales for several years, first saw a Correct Craft ski boat at a Christian camp in Gaylord, Michigan. "He made up his mind at the time that some day he would sell Ski Nautiques," says Ralph Meloon, chairman of the board. "When he grew up, he did it."

As owner of the Correct Craft outlet in Riverside, California, Sherwin, like all dealers, signs an exclusive agreement with the company. His outlet can sell all makes of water skis, pontoon boats, personal water craft, and ski accessories. But the only inboard ski boats it will stock are by Correct Craft. That's a common arrangement in the industry.

THANKING LOYAL SUPPLIERS

"Treating them right" also extends to vendors who supply boat accessories to the company. Correct Craft doesn't change its suppliers often, even if a bidder undercuts the cost of a current supplier. The reasons are a healthy suspicion of "deals" and a sense of loyalty to proven vendors.

When a new prospective supplier concludes, "I'll beat anybody's price out there. Tell me what you're paying and I'll beat it," W. N. backs off. "Either I'm paying too much for the item now or this guy will soon go out of business," he says. "I'd rather pay too much for it than to have the guy go out of business and leave me stranded in the middle of the stream. It's proved to be a good policy here."

The company will consider sound offers from potential new vendors, but it has kept several key suppliers for years. "Some main suppliers are very strong with us, and we don't change for change's sake," W. N. says firmly. "We will change for better quality, but we won't change for money."

W. N. believes this approach also prevents surprises. A new supplier could "get your business and then come back and try to raise the prices on you later. Or they may have to cut the quality of the product to deliver their price. . . . Not only would it be bad for the company, but it's ethically not the proper thing to do.

"I think right wins all the time. It costs a little more, but it wins. You sleep better at night, too. . . . I don't want to sound like we deal with bad guys, because we don't. There are temptations out there, though, because maybe they don't do business the way we do. *That* we have to guard against. We have to be very careful in building those relationships.

"If I throw a supplier out of here because the other guy beat his price, I may be hurting three people. I may be hurting the guy who was giving me good value for high dollars; it was a quality product that my customers deserve. I also may hurt the guy that I take the lower price from; and I probably will hurt our own company."

In 1991, the company's marketing area completed a study showing that Correct Craft could save at least $40,000 a year if it switched to new suppliers, and with no loss of quality. W. N. read the report and then thought of his current suppliers. "They have done good things for us," he noted, pointing to their help in keeping inventory costs low. "And I don't want to change just for the sake of money."[2]

In the early '90s, Correct Craft went to an all-fiberglass boat, removing its final remaining wood components. The company contacted fiberglass suppliers for additional fiberglass parts. But it also began a move to make more parts in-house. The firm now makes its own stringers, the long fiberglass beams that provide a boat's structural backbone. One day it hopes to make all fiberglass parts at the factory. The move to building the entire boat on site already is underway. In 1996, about 60 percent of the boat components were built at the plant.

As the company continues the move to greater on-site boatbuilding (and thus greater quality control and less outside expense), it plans to notify suppliers of impending changes.

"Our fiberglass parts vendor, who started with us very small and has grown with us, already knows of our plans," says production chief Elrod. "We have talked with him and counseled him: 'At some point, we hope to be doing everything you're doing. So you need to be trying to secure other business now.'

"That's an example of how the Meloons do *not* do things.

It isn't a thing of, 'Okay, we want to start doing fiberglass parts on July 1, so we'll let him know on May 31.' All of a sudden he's losing a million-dollar account. I've never known them to treat anybody that way.

"Traditional business thinking would be, 'If they know what you're doing, what if they decide to drop you before you drop them?' Or 'What will happen to your quality or your pricing?'"

At Correct Craft, however, management always operates with its suppliers' concerns in mind. "That's the way they do things," Elrod says, "and that's the right way to do things. And that's why I enjoy coming to work here every day."

Notes

1. Robert G. Flood, *On the Waters of the World* (Chicago: Moody, 1989), 9.
2. John S. Tompkins, "These Good Guys Finish First," *Reader's Digest*, June 1992, 141.

Chapter 9
A Family Firm

he Meloon family is known for its devotion to God and
Christian principles. And W. O. and Walt N. are also
known for their candor. So it's only slightly surprising
to hear W. O. declare, "One of the best things I ever did for the
company was to fire Walt. And one of the best things he did was
to come back. While away from us, he learned good business
lessons."

That straightforward manner typifies W. N., too. When
someone asks him, "Isn't it great to work in a family business?"
he quickly replies, "No—baloney!" Some have followed up
with another rhetorical question: "Well, it's great to work in a
Christian business, isn't it?"

W. N.'s answer is the same: "Baloney. One thing I have
finally learned at my age is that the truth will set you free. If it's
baloney, it ain't steak. You accept it for what it is. Being an
employee of a family company in a management position is not
an easy life. It has all kinds of pitfalls and more grief than you
can wave a stick at."

But at the same time, W. N. will tell you he holds both his
father and his uncle in great esteem, respects their abilities, and
gladly receives their input as members of the board of directors. He also deals with other family members who serve

throughout the company and recognizes he must serve their interests as stockholders (99.9 percent of the company's stock is held by the Meloon family). There are disagreements, but there also is camaraderie, a basic understanding of the mission, and a common desire to honor God.

"You cannot have a family-run business and not have problems," says Ralph, W. N.'s uncle and former company president. "But we get on our knees and work things out." Even among the Meloons, tensions existed prior to the bankruptcy. But those tensions seemed to vanish as W. O., Ralph, their wives, and others struggled to set the company on a steady course. Bankruptcy's pressures drew the family into a closely knit unit. While no one with any sense would ask for the experience of bankruptcy, that temporary "peace" was one of its unexpected benefits. On the other hand, perhaps the tension they've had has been one of the keys to the company's success, as they bounce ideas and disagreements off each other along the way to change.

Significantly, for nearly seventy-five years they have succeeded and are the oldest family-owned boat business in America. How did they do it?

"PEOPLE-PERSONS" AND PRODIGALS

The first two presidents were a lot alike. Both enjoyed people. "My grandfather was a real man. He had a great sense of humor; he loved people," W. N. says of Walt C. "He loved accomplishing the impossible. The routine job did not appeal to him. He was always looking for something that nobody else could do. He loved the challenge of trying to figure another way to do it."

Harold Meloon calls his brother Ralph another people-person, warm and friendly. "I wish I could meet people like Ralph does. My dad was that way, too. He never saw a stranger. He'd walk up to anyone and introduce himself."

The third and fourth presidents are also alike. Both are prodigals who left the family business for a time in search of independence and direction. They returned stronger and became more valuable leaders to the company than they might otherwise have been.

W. O. left school in his midteens, far more interested in boats than in books. "I never got good grades," he says, "because I spent all my time drawing boats. I was thinking boats." The family soon put him to work full-time in the plant.

But W. O. became the prodigal son at age seventeen; he joined top rival Jack Dunn Chris-Craft as a distributor in Old Forge, New York, and Daytona Beach, Florida. In Daytona Beach he met Les Johnson, a boatbuilder who yearned to design boats. After a year and a half, W. O. returned home, but not to Correct Craft. He drove trucks, delivering Florida fruit to Baltimore, Philadelphia, and New York. Later he received a call from Johnson, who had joined Sea Phantom boat company and begun designing boats. The company was moving to Palm Beach in southern Florida; would W. O. join him? W. C. gave his approval, but W. O.'s mother dissented. W. O. went.

While in Palm Beach, he "graduated" from the drugstore soda fountain to beer joints and picked up a tobacco pipe along the way. He stayed at Sea Phantom for about one year and learned the boat trade. Then he received a telegram from his parents urging him to come home and take a job that was open. Grasping the wire in one hand, W. O. went out to the boatyard.

"See here," he said to his coworkers. "They finally have discovered they can't do without me at home."

With that attitude, plus a pipe in his mouth, W. O. walked into his mother's kitchen a few days later. As he entered, she walked out. His grandmother, also in the room, stood her ground.

"Walter," she began, "don't you ever do that again. You have broken your mother's heart."

The prodigal quickly matured. He went back to work for the family firm, anchored himself spiritually, and in 1943 became a charter member of Orlando's Christian Businessmen's Committee (CBMC). Equally important, he had become a competent boat designer. He'd had no prior training in mechanical drawing or naval architecture. But as he observed and assisted Les Johnson, he learned how to design boats, including those with inboard engines. When he returned to Correct Craft, he designed all the boats, from the first inboard boat to fifty-foot yachts years later.

Johnson taught W. O. how the hull's shape would affect a boat's performance. "A boat performs a certain way by the shape of the bottom, and he made very plain to me what you did to make the changes," W. O. explains. "I learned how a little change could either ruin the performance of a boat or make it.

"I watched over his shoulder while he was designing boats. He was someone who would help and do things for you." Sadly, his mentor was also an alcoholic. "He had a beautiful family. But he was no good for patterning your life after, by any means," W. O. says.

It turned out that W. O.'s mom had nothing to worry about. Her son had seen the other side of life and rejected it.

THE PRODIGAL AGAIN

Years later W. O. would have his own prodigal in the person of his firstborn son. W. N. joined the company in 1956. During his second year with the firm, his love of cars and racing got him in plenty of trouble.

One day, he received orders to drive from the Orlando headquarters to Oklahoma to deliver boats. When he reached Montgomery, Alabama, he removed the governor from the carburetor "and got that truck up to where there wasn't anything on the road passing me." Now the two-ton International truck with a cabover and three boats in the rear was heading for Ada, Oklahoma, its teenage driver ready "to set a world land-speed record." And, W. N. says today, "with a truck carrying that size load, I almost accomplished it—except I blew up an engine in Vicksburg, Mississippi."

Unfortunately, the truck was leased from Ryder. "Correct Craft could hardly afford me—I'm out there blowing up engines!" W. N. recalls. He had a new engine put in, went to Ada, unloaded the boats, and headed home. With an empty truck and trailer, he cruised to Pensacola, Florida, before engine problems arose once more. "I never checked the oil in the engine," he admits. "I ran it out of oil and blew the second engine as well."

His father was upset, but the entire bill had not yet arrived. Weeks later, though, W. N. would have a scrape with the law. "I ran with a group here in Pine Castle," he explains. "We weren't criminals; we were just wild. We used to put drag pipes on the cars." He had built a "Fordjillac," putting a 325-horse-power Cadillac engine in a Ford and welding the differentials together. Some police cruisers were constructed similarly, giving them an edge when they chased lawbreakers. W. N. and his friends wanted to stay one step ahead, so they had built their own Fordjillacs.

One night, with his car parked at a corner gas station, W. N. raced the engine with the drag pipes open. The exhaust went straight out instead of through the muffler, and the unrestricted flow "gave the car great pickup and zip, but it also made a lot of noise and so was illegal," W. N. says.

For months, a couple of Pine Castle patrolmen had watched W. N. and his teenage friends, occasionally giving chase, sometimes ignoring, other times issuing warnings. Once in a while they caught a teenage hot-rodder and arrested him; his father would have to come and bail the boy out. The patrolmen considered the boys a bit reckless, but not big-time trouble. One officer, however, viewed them as junior "gangsters" and, says W. N., wanted "to straighten us up."

That night at the gas station, "when I saw that patrolman coming, I shut the engine off. He pulled into the station and told me to start the engine. I told him no, that I didn't have to and wasn't going to do it. He could have arrested me then except that all the guys I ran with kind of ambled up in this crowd and there were just more there than he wanted to bite off. So he said, 'All right, but I'll get you,' and he walked off.

"And he did. He caught me going home one night. He ran up on me with the bright lights on, but without the red lights flashing. Basically, he was just baiting me into doing what I finally did. I'd run up to the stoplight and slam the brakes on, trying to get him to hit me. I thought it was somebody playing with me—one of my friends or one of the boys from the air force base.

"So he kept on, and after four lights I thought, *I'm tired of playing this game. I'm going home.* So I pulled the lever on the tailpipe, popped the overdrive, and took off as the light turned green. The minute I did, there were his lights flashing. I thought, *Well, I'm in this deep; we're going to go for it.* So I did. I ran."

Eventually the patrolman cornered Meloon. He charged the teen with speeding, reckless driving, and resisting arrest. From the sheriff's station, W. N. called his father.

W. O. came to the station and posted bail for his son. The bail totaled $250, a major amount for a teen in 1957. Though his father paid it, W. N. "had to sell everything I had to pay my father back for that."

The arrest and paying of bail did not get W. N. fired. But a week later, when the final bills showed up for the truck repairs in Montgomery and Pensacola, W. N. was in jeopardy. "This was not a real good situation," he says simply. The final straw, according to his father, was when he came into his son's office one day to find W. N.'s feet propped up on the desk. W. O. had warned his son about it several times; to the father, it represented a bad attitude of laziness and smug self-satisfaction. Combined with the truck and car incidents, it finally led W. O. to fire his son.

Away from the family business, W. N. learned major lessons about responsibility and, equally important, how to help a business flourish. A Correct Craft executive, Norman Sewell, referred him to a friend in personnel at Martin Marietta, the defense contractor (now Martin-Lockheed). Thus began a five-year stint that would help to mature the young rebel.

As one of the first 1,400 employees to work at Martin, W. N. did federal catalog work, checking prices and parts in stock. The catalog department soon was consolidated, and W. N. hoped to join another part of the company. At the interview, Claude Gilley, big, redheaded, and Irish, asked him, "Why do you want to work for me?"

"Frankly, I'd like to have your job," answered the young Meloon with typical candor.

"Fine," Gilley said. "I'll train you for my job if you want. And I'll tell you why I'm going to do that. I've been lookin' for somebody who wants my job, because I want to advance. When my boss comes down and says, 'How long will it take you to train somebody and move up?' I don't want to wait two weeks [the normal training time]. If I have to wait two weeks to get that other job, they may change their mind, or they may find somebody else, and I don't start earnin' the higher salary the other two weeks. That's crazy. I want to say to him, 'Boss, I can move today, because Walt knows my job as well as I do.'

"The other reason is this: If I get hit by a truck tomorrow and I can't come to work, I have done a disservice to this company if I haven't trained somebody to do my job so that this company doesn't miss me."

W. N. had never considered that perspective before. "But it made a lot of sense to me as to what an employee's obligation is to a company, especially in a management position," he says. "When you do that, the company owes you more than just a few weeks' salary or some benefit. The company is indebted to you more then. You're much more valuable."

Like his father, W. N. now had found a teacher and mentor. As Les Johnson had taught boat design to W. O. years before, now Claude Gilley taught W. N. about sound business practices. "He had the biggest effect on me," W. N. acknowledges. "He probably taught me more than anyone else." When W. N. returned to the family business, the practical knowledge learned through Gilley had balanced two years of junior college business courses, making him much more valuable to Correct Craft.

He returned with a new humility, and with a wife and two young children to feed. "We can't afford to pay you a lot, but we can pay you what they're paying," W. O. said as he made his son the job offer. "But it's probably going to seem like less because you're going to have to work harder. You have to understand that whatever you have to do to complete the work, you must do. If you can commit to that, we'd like to have you come back to work."

W. N. had learned many things while away, and now he wanted to help the company. He returned despite the bankruptcy, which at times put his paychecks in jeopardy. "The first eight weeks I didn't cash my paychecks because of the company's financial limits," he says. "Other family members also chose not to cash their checks because of limited cash flow. But I had anticipated that."

W. N. continued to mature in his business skills even as the company grew, and he became general manager in 1979, handling, by his estimate, 85 percent of daily operations. In 1985, he became the fourth president in the firm's history.

CHALLENGES AT A FAMILY-RUN COMPANY

W. N. views his position as a calling: "I have felt that I was called to do this job as much as a preacher is called to preach." His goal remains to glorify God and, secondarily, to make money for the business and stockholders. Family members direct three of the five regional warehouses. Two other relatives are members of the board of directors, and the three most recent presidents are all sons and grandsons of the founder. At times that puts unique pressures on the president. As a loving family member, he wants to please relatives even as he protects company interests.

"I have to review a decision in terms of 'This individual is a family member; this individual is also a stockholder of this company; and this individual is also a customer through the warehouse operations.' Often when I make a decision to protect the interests of stockholders, it's at 180 degrees variance from what the family member thinks I should do for him as a customer."

As W. N. tries to balance those three relationships, he also wants to "wrap it up in what is spiritually the correct way to handle the situation." He admits that at times "it's very difficult. How many decisions can you make that are right when you have to consider those three aspects and apply the Scriptures to all of them?"

W. O. acknowledges that tensions existed on and off during his presidency as well. Working with family members, he says, requires greater understanding and the tolerating by family of "things you wouldn't let anyone else do. I look back at Scripture and see that Joseph had the same problem with jealousy."

W. N. deals with the tensions and disagreements several ways. He receives good counsel; he has a friendship with Christian businessman and consultant Harry Cohn, who advises him on ethical and business matters. He also respects his elders. Both his father and his uncle are board members and past presidents, and they offer their perspectives, which he considers carefully.

"Scripturally, more than just being older, they're my elders, and Scripture teaches . . . that I should honor and respect that. And I do, and I have to bite my tongue sometimes to do it. . . . I wouldn't take anything for the family. There isn't enough money in the world to make it worthwhile to throw the family over and just say nuts to their ideas. Yet there are other days when I don't want to hear them. But that's the job I have. When I mess it up the most is when I'm not in tune with what God wants done around here.

"And it causes a whole lot of grief," W. N. notes. Although he listens to W. O. and Ralph, as the president he chooses sometimes not to follow their recommendations, and he doesn't always tell them of his disagreement. That, he says, creates further guilt and tension.

"It places a tremendous amount of guilt on an individual, when I should probably look at Dad and say, 'Dad, I appreciate what you said, but I can't do it that way and I'm not going to do it that way.'" But he declines to be so direct "because I just don't want to go through the hassle of it. . . . If I had been honest in the first place, I'd be over with it; you're not carrying the baggage around anymore."

Still, he welcomes their input. "These men bring a tremendous amount of knowledge. There are still many things they bring in here that are helpful and give me perspective. I know beyond a shadow of a doubt that if it weren't for both of those men and my grandfather—had these men not put in their fifty-six years and had my grandfather not put in his fifty years —I wouldn't be sitting here."

W. N. believes that God used many things, including the bankruptcy, to bring the company to its present position, and he views change as good, assuming it honors the company's vision. "As long as something keeps working, fine. . . . But there does come a time when changes need to be made. You can still stay within the boundaries, but maybe you have to change the rules a bit. . . . . In athletics, the rules evolve over the years. But they have boundaries, or principles. When you get to that principle, or sideline, you stop. We do the same thing."

In addition to seeking good counsel and honoring his elders, W. N. handles family tensions by making sure his management team remains neutral, supporting the company rather than any individual. He also tells a prospective manager to remember the company is family run and to respect all family members. "And in doing that," W. N. explains, "you cannot defend my position in an argument with my family. Never get between me and the family. If they ask you a question about me, answer the question. But if it gets argumentative, stop talking. Do not defend my policies or my position to members of my family that you have to work with every day."

The final way he handles family tensions is through his spiritual life, calling on God's help. "When I don't take time to let God help me with it, I mess it up," he says. "But that's understandable. When I can keep it in the guidelines of the spiritual, it's much easier to handle the issues.

"Usually I don't touch it. God takes care of it. But being president of the company, there's a certain human nature about me. 'Hey, I'm the president of the company!' Oops. When I do that, I just got out of step with God."

Over the years, W. N. has become a respected leader of the company and the sport of waterskiing. He has served as president of the American Water Ski Educational Foundation. He attends many tournaments and encourages young skiers through Correct Craft's sponsorship program (see chapter 11).

A FAMILY TRADITION

Other third-generation Meloons have contributed to the company's success as well. Ken Meloon, Ralph's younger son, directs both Midwest Correct Craft and Southwest Correct Craft. As one of the earliest warehouse operations, Midwest has prospered in sales. It and Southwest had combined annual sales of $16 million in the mid 1990s. Ken has directed the Midwest operation since 1974, building the territory and managing it wisely. A man of deep spiritual commitment, he serves in a Bible-believing local church and seeks to glorify God with the resources He has bountifully supplied. Ken echoes his father's conviction that God honors those who honor Him.

Ralph Jr., Ken's older brother, is a former president of Pacific Coast Correct Craft and now serves as a hunting and fishing guide and owner of Harbor Terrace Inn Bed and Breakfast in Soldonta, Alaska. He is committed to missions and in 1995 accompanied Samaritan's Purse president Franklin Graham to Rwanda. There he helped and observed the mission agency's work in a hospital and orphanage. The story appeared in *Decision* magazine.[1]

A fourth generation of Meloons is active in the company as well, including W. O.'s grandsons Jeff Warner and Gary Meloon (W. N.'s son). Jeff operates the archives and customer service and leads daily tours at the company headquarters, which include a visit to the boat factory to watch workers building the latest Ski Nautiques. Gary is materials manager, directing purchasing, distribution, and inventory at the factory; he reports to production vice president Mike Elrod. A mentoring relationship exists there, which greatly pleases W. N.

"My son has a relationship with a man who is not only his boss but is also his elder," W. N. says. "He's also his mentor. . . . Mike is able to help form this young man for the future. He brings to Gary a philosophy and a principle, a direction, and a commitment that may be wrong for me to force on my son. I could ruin his chances for the rest of his life because I'm his father if I'm not careful how I do it. I understand that."

As a fourth-generation Meloon and son of the president, Gary seems a likely candidate to eventually succeed his father. Yet that's not automatic; any decision would come from the board of directors. W. N. believes there may be other capable leaders within the company. But he does want his son to know the company well, and he's seeing to Gary's training through Mike Elrod and others.

Gary also has a strong relationship with one of W. N.'s best friends, Don Purdy, from Camp of the Woods. "A child always needs to have a relationship with adults other than a mother and father," W. N. says, "—on a business basis, a recreational basis, and a spiritual basis."

A FAMILY THAT'S FIRM IN RESPECT

The three most recent presidents respect one another's strengths yet are able to recognize their weaknesses. In their evaluations, the love and esteem for one another is apparent.

W. N. describes Ralph as "a number cruncher" and "a money manager," skilled at "making numbers work." Ralph acknowledges those skills and calls himself "a natural businessman and a natural mathematician." He calculated most government contracts for W. C. and W. O. during their leadership. "I always counted my costs, and I always was on the conservative side," Ralph adds. Lately Ralph has become a goodwill ambassador, traveling abroad to ski tournaments to promote both waterskiing and the company. Approaching eighty, he is always ready to tell a story and declare the goodness of God in his life.

"Over the years, he has developed this ambassador identity, and he's doing very well at it," W. N. says. "He's good at it because he likes to travel, he likes to be around people, he likes to tell them stories, and he has that draw. It has been very good for the company."

Ralph's weakness was W. O.'s strength. "Walt's not only a great boatbuilder, but he's also a great visionary," Ralph says. As an example, he mentions his brother's decision to invite all the dealers to the Orlando headquarters. At the time, no other boat company had brought all its dealers together for a corporate meeting. And W. O. decided to build Correct Craft's first recreational fiberglass boat, the Classic, after the government contract for 3,000 assault boats had soured W. C. on using fiberglass.

"We've been a great team," Ralph believes. "I've been the action person; Walt's been the visionary. I'm a realist. I knew the payroll had to be met. He's the dreamer. He's like Joseph in the Bible, seeing how things could be done."

W. O.'s humility about leading the company back from bankruptcy has impressed Van Thurston, the director of Turnaround Ministries. God certainly helped, but He worked through a willing servant, Thurston believes. Meanwhile, W. N. appreciates other qualities evident during W. O.'s presidency and even today, especially compassion and generosity. "My father is a very caring, loving, giving individual," W. N. says. "He will give himself into oblivion—financially and every other way.

"Dad also had tremendous insight into boat design and planing hulls. He knew what would make them perform well and what would make them perform poorly, be it a softer-riding boat, be it a faster-riding boat, be it a flatter-running boat. Over the years, he has had a tremendous insight into that area."

Though W. O. can be direct at times, most who know him commend him as tactful and gracious. In contrast, W. N. considers himself more direct. "I'm a very direct, black-and-white kind of a person," he says. "Don't try to make an end run around me. If you're going to go at me, come right down the middle. I take things head-on.

"I'm a high D [dominant] temperament. Sometimes I get headstrong. I tell my managers, 'Guys, if I am pushing you in a direction you're not comfortable going in, I will fire you if you don't come in here and tell me how you feel. I'll never fire you if you look me straight in the face and say, "Walt, you're about to mess this thing up."'

"I want people who are capable of standing their ground, being strong, and following their convictions. I've had a couple of men I've come down on pretty hard. They stayed in the chair and looked me straight in the face and told me, 'Look, you're wrong.' Then I've had to do some soul-searching real quick. I either had to stay on course and they had to conform to it, or . . . I had to buy into what they were saying."

If W. N.'s weakness is his sometimes-blunt approach, his strength is his ability to manage and plan. As his father says, "He's very efficient, having divided the company into eight departments, each with its own budget. They have weekly management meetings." W. O. describes his own management style as democratic compared to his son's authoritarian approach, but he adds, "I've tried not to be too critical. I have never sold in any one year within $10 million worth of the boats my son has. Evidently, he's not wrong." Ralph also applauds W. N.'s organizational skills.

On one thing the three men stand united: Correct Craft must continue to make quality boats for the glory of God.

Note
1. Ralph C. Meloon Jr., "The Trip That Changed My Life," *Decision*, August 1995, 28–29.

Chapter 10
Fiberglass Boats

*O*ver the years, Correct Craft's recreational line has ranged from speed boats and fishing boats to fifty-foot yachts. W. C. began with outboard engines, but as he started to build ski boats in earnest, he left the outboards that had powered his racing boats, trading speed boats for wake-performance boats. The Tournament Skier, for example, developed in the late 1940s, was an all-mahogany inboard. And the Atom Skier, a compact fourteen-feet, two-inch runabout, is considered a '50s classic, still maintained by many boat lovers more than forty years after its introduction.[1]

In its heyday, the little Atom cranked out forty-five horse-power and reached speeds of thirty-eight miles per hour. It first appeared in 1951, making it one of the first inboard ski boats.[2] One Atom Skier remains on display at the Water Ski Hall of Fame.

Correct Craft entered the fiberglass era in 1960 with the Classic, a seventeen-foot towboat. A year later it developed its second fiberglass entry, the Mustang, with a narrower hull and sixteen-foot length. But the recent bankruptcy had taken its toll: Correct Craft had limited funds for development and marketing of these new craft. And at first W. O. and Ralph didn't tell their retired father about the new fiberglass craft, knowing he wanted no more fiberglass after the contract for 3,000 fiberglass boats a couple years earlier helped lead the company to bankruptcy.

In spring 1961, a Miami ski-school operator named Leo Bentz approached Correct Craft, offering to sell the mold to his fiberglass boat and rights to the name for $10,000. Bentz had contracted with a local boatbuilder the previous year to build a new ski boat with a hull designed for a smoother wake. Bentz was neither a boat designer nor a marketer; he was a prelaw student operating three ski schools. Yet he had sold all twelve of the boats built for him, including one to future Hall of Famer Wayne Grimditch. The boat was gaining acceptance among top tournament skiers.[3]

With a fiberglass boat of its own, Correct Craft saw little need to add a second to the lineup. And with the bankruptcy, "at that point we couldn't have paid $10,000 for anything," W. O. says.

Almost a year later, Bentz returned to Pine Castle, but Meloon saw him coming and tried to head him off in the street. "Leo, I'm in no better position than I was months ago," W. O. said.

"I haven't come to sell my boat but to *give* it to you," Bentz answered.

And so he had. Bentz offered the molds without charge, as well as use of the name *Ski Nautique.* In return, he required only that Correct Craft supply him one new boat a year for three years and provide free service to all the boats he had already sold. With those terms, W. O. relented.

Bentz's bargain was driven by concern for his pregnant wife and continued demand for his boats. He had let his orders be filled by any boatbuilder willing to quickly assemble two or three at a time, and the quality had suffered. Correct Craft represented his major hope of keeping the boat alive, strengthening his schools with new boats, and providing free repairs for his boats already sold.

Correct Craft agreed to the deal "if for no other reason than to get him off our backs," says W. N. "Then when we were testing one of his boats, we found out that it ran pretty well."[4]

Thus began Correct Craft's vaunted Ski Nautique, a name that's now been around for more than thirty-five years, and the maiden boat in the modern inboard ski boat industry. *Ski Nautique* in French means "water ski." Notes *Trailer Boats* magazine, "The Ski Nautique is arguably the most recognized name worldwide."[5]

One driver came back from test runs with the Ski Nautique and noted, "It doesn't look great, but from seventy-five feet back, it handles well." Skiers holding the towrope liked the ride. The wake behind the boat was superior to that of Correct Craft's own Classic and Mustang.

Though the first model was rough, with rakish angles, legendary tournament driver Jack Walker recalls, "My first thought was, *We've come a long way, baby.* He was impressed with the ease of handling. "This was something your wife and kids could drive. For those days, it was comfortable and nice-looking."[6]

After building fifty Ski Nautiques, Correct Craft's mold had virtually disintegrated. Bentz had discarded the plug for the mold, so an entirely new mold had to be made. When the plug maker came for measurements on the old mold, he discovered one side was an inch wider at the keel. "Which side do you want me to build?" he asked. W. O. said to use the wider side, which effectively added one inch to the other.

The Meloons decided it was time to improve the product. They modified the design, especially the deck. W. O. eliminated the annoying beam that ran across the width of the interior. The beam had served as a seat back, a place to attach the ski rope, and a cross beam to hold the boat together. But it also kept the driver and passenger from easily getting from the front to the back of the boat. W. O. also added a pylon near midship to attach the towrope, better throttle controls, and rear-facing seats so passengers could watch the skier.

THUMBS UP FROM TOURNAMENT SKIERS

When Bentz had described the Nautique's strengths to the Meloons, he had talked about how tournament skiers were embracing the boat. The pros, those passionate skiers at the top of the sport who traveled from one competition to the next, liked the boat's performance. He mentioned tournament favorite Wayne Grimditch in particular. "Bentz's pitch focused on tournament water skiing, and we had no idea what tournament water skiing was all about," admitted W. N. "We couldn't relate to the market."[7]

Now W. O. decided the interest among the pros was worth pursuing, and he contacted Bill Clifford, the executive director of the American Water Ski Association (AWSA), for advice on how to spur more interest and better promote the boat. "He told me the skiers had to ask for it," says W. O., who asked Clifford for a list of fifteen of the top competitive skiers. Correct Craft then offered everyone on the list a new Ski Nautique at half price if they would use it and take it to tournaments. Fourteen of the fifteen took the company up on the deal.

Clifford, executive director of AWSA for twenty-seven years,[8] believed part of the company's success with its new fiberglass boat was due to timing. "It's important to note that the sport was coming of age, and the Meloons were definitely in the right place at the right time," he said. But he also noted the Meloons' willingness to do something new. "Just as importantly, they *listened.* I think that's the success story."[9]

Discounting boats 50 percent to promote sales while potential bankruptcy loomed was controversial. "People within my own organization thought I was nuts," W. O. says, "because we were right on the edge of bankruptcy. But I guess there are just some things it's easier to apologize for than to get permission."[10] And the strategy of putting the boats into the hands of pro skiers succeeded far beyond the president's expectations.

"That's been the basis for its popularity," W. O. says. The boat began to show up at all the water-ski tournaments, and everywhere water-skiers live, from San Diego to Maine. Correct Craft was the first to do it; now most ski boat makers have their own tournament teams, champion skiers who receive discounted boats and often free accessories in exchange for promotional considerations. And the initial offer of half-price boats helped competitive skiers at a time when money purses were light. "I think that's had a lot to do with waterskiing's fast growth," W. O. says.

Today the company sponsors between fifteen and twenty outstanding skiers, as well as winning wakeboarders. They're all part of Team Nautique, men and women chosen for their accomplishments, overall attitude, and popularity with competitors and the public. In 1996, Team Nautique had twenty members. Correct Craft provides the skiers with a towboat at discount and free service. In return, some skiers appear at boat shows and clinics representing the company. All the skiers, as active tournament entrants, generate positive publicity for Correct Craft boats as they compete and often win.

RESEARCH AND DEVELOPMENT

Members of Team Nautique also give valuable feedback on the product's performance. They're part of the company's devotion to improving the boat with advances in design and technology. Research and development (R&D) took off under W. O.'s leadership. A continuing program of testing and research finds staff opening the throttle on Lakes Jessamine and Conway, which flank Correct Craft headquarters. W. N. calls their modern R&D program "Dad's brainchild. He came up with the idea, and that got the creative juices of all our design people flowing. We've kept the competitive skiers involved and used them to test the results of any changes we've made. We get suggestions from them, as well as ideas from our own people."

"We've spent a lot of money developing new ideas," adds Ralph Meloon. "Also, we've brought a lot of people up in the company, which is important. And anything we've done that's been good has been with God's help."[11]

Those developments began to pay real dividends in several areas, including one that helps skiers the most, wake performance. The boat's wake has become smoother over the years, helping recreational and tournament skiers alike have smoother rides with less spray and bounce. That doesn't mean the early models weren't helping skiers. The boat "already had 'rideability' and lower wakes," W. O. says. But they wanted to improve the product, and despite the financial constraints in place, they were able to do so. "When we started to get some money coming in, we began to experiment. An example is the rudders. We learned a long time ago they have a lot more to do with a boat's performance than people think. Just a couple minutes of grinding the rudder would make the boat steer perfectly.

"We also widened the boat in the late '60s and curled the bottom down and out to keep the spray from passing into the boat. Then we also dropped a deeper V in the hull."[12]

By 1970, the Ski Nautique had stretched to seventeen feet, eleven inches and featured a redesigned deck, making it much more stylish. Today the boat is nineteen feet, six inches from bow to stern.

The greatest series of refinements came in the 1990s. Indeed, Correct Craft marketers have called the 1990 changes "revolutionary." A new hull design added almost a foot to the length and widened the boat six inches overall. Designers also inserted grooves, or channels, in the hull to direct the spray downward rather than outward toward the skier. These "spray relief pockets" appeared near the chine—the point where the hull side meets the hull bottom—and yielded a smoother, quieter ride.

Design engineer Bruce Borden likes to compare the effect of the channels to a kid's fingers moving through Jell-O. "Stick a finger into Jell-O and pull it across, and you create a trough. That's what we did; we created a trough across the bottom, just inside the chine."

The 1990 model introduced two other major changes: computer technology in the engine and "reverse chines" on the hull. The PleasureCraft Marine engine contained the first electronic engine management system programmed specifically for ski boats. The computer module helped performance by giving faster acceleration, greater maximum speed, and increased fuel efficiency. Meanwhile, designers took the flat edge of the chine and angled it downward, reducing the wake further.

The other major change in the 1990s came with Total Surface Control (TSC), a series of design changes and a new progressive pitch propeller (see chapter 11). TSC represented innovative hull design and debuted with the 1997 models.

The Ski Nautique has became the flagship of the modern Correct Craft fleet. In 1997, four models of Nautiques were offered: the Sport Nautique, Nautique Super Sport, the compact Ski Nautique 176, and the Ski Nautique itself.

FINDING FIBERGLASS TREES

When the new fiberglass ski boats made their first appearance, perhaps the only one associated with the company not gung ho about them was company founder W. C. Meloon. Besides having bad memories about the government contract gone awry in the late 1950s, W. C. was a traditionalist. He had been reared on the qualities of wood and had heard the customers' praises for the mahogany Tournament Skier and Atom Skier models. In his view, fiberglass seemed to contradict the laws of nature. As Walter N. put it, "According to W. C., there were no fiberglass trees, so that wasn't the way to go."[13]

In fact, in 1960 a number of critics wondered if fiberglass would withstand water, weather, age, stress, and speed.[14]

Correct Craft built its first fiberglass boat while the founder was at the New Hampshire warehouse, certain that if W. C. had been back at the Florida headquarters, he would have fought the venture. "He never would've allowed it if he were here," W. N. says. "So we sent him one, with no explanation, and the truck driver said, 'Mr. Meloon, wait until you see the new fiberglass boat they've built.' We would've liked to have seen the look on his face at that moment!"

Notes

1. One owner of a 1954 Atom Skier installed a new engine and transmission and laminated mahogany over the plywood deck. (The original Atom Skier was rich mahogany.) The couple call it "a fun little boat." See "Frisks Launch 1954 Atom Skier," *Nautique News,* fall/winter 1996, 2.
2. Robert Stephens, "Evolution and Revolution," *Water Ski,* February 1995, 47.

3. Zenon Bilas, "The History of the Inboard Waterski Boat," *Trailer Boats,* February 1996, 38.
4. Jim Harmon, "The Meloons: Three Parts Know-How, Three Parts Faith," *Powerboat,* August 1982, 46.
5. Bilas, "The History of the Inboard Waterski Boat," 39.
6. Stephens, "Evolution and Revolution," 48.
7. Harmon, "The Meloons," 47.
8. William D. Clifford was executive director from 1958–85. He died in 1989 and is a member of the Water Ski Hall of Fame.
9. Harmon, "The Meloons," 47.
10. Ibid.
11. Ibid., 60.
12. Stephens, "Evolution and Revolution," 49.
13. Ibid.
14. Bilas, "The History of the Inboard Waterski Boat," 38.

Chapter 11
Quality Counts

*J*n 1987, a *Popular Mechanics* test team put six inboard ski boats through a series of acceleration and handling tests at Cypress Gardens and declared the Ski Nautique 2001 "the boat the test team would like to own." Citing the "soft ride, near-perfect handling and exceptional fit and finish," it named the Correct Craft towboat its test winner. In 1994, the Ski Nautique again took top honors, the magazine calling the boat "the overall *PM* test favorite." It tied for first in both slalom wake characteristics and in fit and finish; it was second in performance course time.

Popular Mechanics also hailed the 1994 Nautique for its handling in choppy water. "Gale-like conditions forced us to run the Nautique in a huge chop one day, and we can report that in addition to being an outstanding slalom performer, it has one of the best rough-water rides in the test."[1]

Correct Craft Nautiques have done well in other industry tests, too, including one by *Water Ski* magazine, but the *PM* findings are especially notable because the publication receives no advertising from the boating industry that might influence its evaluations. World-class slalom skier Susi Graham held the towrope during the 1994 test; behind the wheel of the Correct Craft entry was someone who knew the boat well, Scott Mohr.

The firm's field marketing and promotions manager, he got excited at the less-than-ideal conditions on Lake Sheen in Windermere, Florida. Mohr was convinced the Nautique would show its stuff and overcome the wave action, smoothing the way for Graham.

"It was a windy day," he remembers. "We were loving it, because we knew there would be a lot of chop." One reason the Nautique calmed the waters was its deep relief pockets that channel spray away from the chine (where the side of the hull meets the hull bottom).

BETTER BOATS

Building better boats has always been a primary goal of the firm, dating back to company founder W. C. Meloon. President W. N. Meloon wrote in the 1997 catalog, "[W. C.'s] tenet for doing business was very basic, 'Offer your customer the best product, the finest materials and build it to the glory of God.'"

Better materials and design are two ways the company succeeds at building quality boats. For instance, the boatbuilder uses special, environmentally friendly resin. Called AME 5000, this epoxy resin is less likely to deteriorate in the water over time than the more common polyester resins used in boat making. "The environment is important to us, but our concern is always quality first," Mohr explains. "Epoxy resin is stronger and more durable. Polyester resins can crack or pull apart during the drying process or much later during continual exposure." Using AME 5000 costs about $1.50 more per pound. The average 800-pound hull contains 400 pounds of resin.

In its designs, the company uses four stringers instead of two. Stringers, made of aluminum and fiberglass, form the backbone of the hull and run from bow to stern and side to side, giving the hull stability. The company also has added reverse angles to the chine to help channel spray downward. Correct Craft was not the first company to have these two innovations. American Skier, for example, introduced four stringers instead of two, keeping the hull stable through rough waters. American Skier's Ken Elkind also altered previously parallel chines. "By reversing them, the water would be deflected down. It worked; the boat immediately had more lift and stability."[2]

As in those two cases, Correct Craft doesn't always pioneer new developments. But it often improves on established technology. W. N. explains the business attitude toward change: "We don't make change for change's sake." The firm delayed adopting fiberglass stringers for several years until "we knew more about it, understood it, and could make glass stringer that we could fill with foam and then . . . make the stringers a part of the boat, not set them in a compound or a glue—something like that—as separate units that you hope stick together. We wanted them to be a permanent part of the boat."

Correct Craft stringers are bonded to the boat exclusively with fiberglass, a more expensive but stronger adhesive than glues or other compounds many rivals use. Similarly, the AME 5000 resin was introduced by another manufacturer, and several boatbuilders use it on the outer skin. But Correct Craft is one of only a few boatbuilders that make the whole boat out of AME 5000.

Reflecting its commitment to improving existing technology, the company has increased the angle on the reverse chines on its 1997 Ski Nautique. The greater angle reduces the amount of spray behind the boat, which helps skiers on a shorter towline. Several other refinements to the 1997 model have earned that boat's design the term "revolutionary" (see "Total Surface Control").

SIGNIFICANT INNOVATIONS

Along the way, Correct Craft has introduced a couple of significant firsts itself. The company developed the first ski pylon in the early 1950s. Until then, the towrope was attached at the back of the boat to a lift ring, one of two rings used to lift the boat out of the water. (A few boatbuilders later made a separate part with a small indentation for wrapping the towrope.)

But located so close to the stern, the ring gave larger skiers undue influence on the boat.

"A heavy skier could control the direction of the boat. If pulled off to one side, he could do it," explains W. O. Meloon. Like a child on a skateboard who latches onto the back of a friend's bike and then pulls to one side, making the bike's end slide, a skier could cause the boat to veer from its straight course by moving quickly to one side of the wake. The Meloons changed the tow attachment to a post, or pylon, and placed the pylon just ahead of the inboard engine and much closer to the center of the boat.

"It was practically in the middle of the boat in length and also in weight distribution," W. O. adds. "The skier could no longer affect the direction of the boat." The new position allowed slalom skiing to thrive. In slalom competition, skiers come within six inches of buoys as they weave across a course, moving sharply from side to side. Now instead of pulling down on the boat's stern, the skiers put their force just behind the boat's center, where the pylon absorbs the shock without the skiers' tugging the boats. Other boat makers soon adopted the pylon and its position near midship.

Correct Craft also developed the first tracking fin for inboard ski boats. Tracking fins were common for old outboard racing boats before waterskiing, and Correct Craft also had fins on its line of fishing outboards. The company introduced tracking fins to its towboats with the Ski Nautique.

As the name suggests, the fin allows the boat to stay on track, holding a straight line down a slalom course or a course leading to a ski jump. Without the fin, the boat would slide sideways. With it, the boat "grips" the course.

QUALITY VERSUS PROFITS

Quality counts at Correct Craft, company officials say. Many factors affect profits besides the number of boats built; government regulations, vendor costs, and competition are only three. But profit levels are always secondary to quality.

"In our society, there's a lot of people and companies that don't care how they achieve profits; they just want the bottom-line profits," explains production vice president Mike Elrod. "The Meloons aren't that way. Sure, they like to make money. But they won't cut corners to do it. The quality of the product we build is second to none. What we put in the parts of the boat you don't see is just as good as what you do see. A lot of companies don't do that. I think that contributes to their longevity and their stability."

Correct Craft has produced as many as one-third of all inboard ski boats sold in a given year. Yet President W. N. Meloon argues that competitors' sales and methods don't drive the company's decisions. "I do make decisions based on what they do, but that cannot be the ruling factor," he says. "As a Christian and the head of this company, I can't let that persuade me in making decisions. When numbers and money become the motivating factors of this company, it's wrong."

Like any good businessperson, W. N. wants the multimillion-dollar company to continue to increase its revenues. "I don't think it's wrong to want greater revenue and profit," he says. "What could be wrong is how we get there. You make a decision based on the right way to get there."

The right way includes a quality product using quality materials. Elrod explains the company's strong, stable sales in the 1990s this way: "Once we've got the potential customer in the product and he finds out how good it runs, how solid it feels, and the beautiful wake behind it, he gives it a long look." And the company's "being in business for more than seventy years and how we have treated people" gives it a good reputation among customers, he adds.

TOTAL SURFACE CONTROL

Part of building a quality product involves an innovative hull design for 1997. With it, Correct Craft expects to gain market share. In addition to the modified reverse angle chine, the hull has enhanced spray relief pockets, a streamlined bow, and a tapered transom, as well as a new keel relief pocket. All help to redirect the water flow over the hull, giving a low and smoother wake, which skiers like, and improved tracking for easier handling, which drivers appreciate. A new progressive-pitch, four-blade propeller to increase acceleration is the final design change in a package the company calls Total Surface Control (TSC).

The four-blade propeller replaces the three-blade as the standard driving force. Why the change after all these years? A four-blade typically loses speed on the high end, and recreational boaters like speed. But because a four-blade offers quicker acceleration and a smoother and quieter ride, Correct Craft wondered if a four-blade could be developed that could deliver good top speed. "So we issued a challenge to our prop supplier to retain the speed," says Bill Snook, the engineering/design manager.

"Let's work together. We'll test them and tell you the results," Snook told their California vendor. "Let's get this prop to where it doesn't pull back on speed." The California company shipped several variations of a new four-blade design, finally finding a winning design in a progressive-pitch propeller. The progressive pitch makes the propeller more efficient, increasing thrust. Correct Craft was the second boatbuilder to adopt the four-blade propeller. But it was the first to use progressive pitch to increase thrust.

The new propeller was "better accelerating, smoother, quieter, and had the same top speed as the three-blade prop," according to Snook. The boat still reaches forty-six miles per hour (MPH).

Another major innovation in the TSC package was the keel relief pocket, a clever indentation dug just behind the keel. Borden Larson, supervisor of new product development and a designer, calls the indentation a "divot" that "knocks down the rooster tail" that usually shoots up from the keel. As in developing the progressive-pitch propeller, the company devised the clever divot after much testing.

Using trial and error, "sticking a finger in the water here and there, seeing how it improved the shape of the wake," Snook says, Correct Craft developed an indentation that channeled water downward. The relief pocket lowers the pressure coming off the transom, and a lesser volume of water funnels to the tail. The result is a smaller, less turbulent rooster tail and a smoother ride.

Early returns indicated a big thumbs up from skiers, and even some world records. Kristi Overton Johnson has won several tournament skiing titles and in 1996 was the women's slalom world record holder. Skiing behind a new 1997 Ski Nautique just weeks after the boat's debut, she set a new slalom world record of 1 buoy missed at 41 feet off the towline. That means she skied around 1 buoy with only 34 feet of line. (The average line is 75 feet, and Kristi skied with 41 feet off that line.) That destroyed her previous record of 4 buoys at 39 1/2 feet off.[3] At the same tournament in Miami Beach, both the boys (ages nine and less) and boys III (thirteen to sixteen) winners set new world records in the ski jump, and Brenda Nichols set a national jump record for women's II (ages twenty-five to thirty-four).

RAVE REVIEWS

Other boats in the 1997 fleet have also won rave reviews. The newest model, the Ski Nautique 176, is exactly two feet shorter than the Ski Nautique and includes the same four-blade propeller, spray relief pockets, and AME 5000 resin components. Priced at almost $8,000 less than the Ski Nautique, the 176 has been called "value-packed" by one reviewer. "The manufacturer . . . absolutely doesn't skimp in attention to quality or skiability," the reviewer wrote in *Trailer Boats* magazine. The smaller boat "accommodates boaters with small garages who want to store their boats at home. It's also ideal for boaters who visit lakes with size restrictions and for people who simply don't need the additional length."[4]

Meanwhile, the Sport Nautique, first introduced in 1989, continues to be a favorite among wakeboarders as well as skiers. Correct Craft made its reputation with water-skiers, but it has gained a name among wakeboarders with its sport version. The Sport Nautique has been the official towboat for the Wakeboard World Championships and the U.S. Wakeboard Open in both 1995 and 1996, as well as the Wakeboard Masters and U. S. National Wakeboarding Championship. It was the official towboat of the first competitive wakeboard tournament in Kauai in 1990 and has pulled most world competitions since. And the Sport Nautique is riding the popularity of wakeboarding, which drew a large media following in the mid-1990s with coverage of the sport on ESPN, ABC-TV's *Good Morning America,* and half a dozen popular magazines. ESPN has called wakeboarding a hot sport of Generation X teens and adults, those born from 1965 to 1984, and has featured wakeboarders and barefoot skiers on its so-called *X Games* coverage.[5]

The Sport Nautique is popular for its precise throttle response and wake characteristics. The boat can go twice as fast, but wakeboarders love it at twenty MPH, where the speed is steady and the wake is defined. On the Sport Nautique, the more-defined wake propels riders along in the minisurf. "The weight and hull design make the difference," says Scott Mohr. At twenty MPH, the wake is "more solid than a 'cut-through' wake" used in the three water-ski events of slalom, jump, and trick. Scott describes the Sport Nautique's wake as "a well-defined ramp that allows the rider to rise off the wake without being pitched out the front or crashing through the wake due to a too-steep wake." He also believes the sport design works with the passenger weight to produce "a larger but not overdeveloped wake" that benefits the wakeboarder.

The fourth 1997 model is the Super Sport Nautique. First introduced in 1995, the Super Sport represents a redesign of the Excel, Correct Craft's first modern V-drive model. Inboard engines typically are placed in midship, making the driver's cockpit separate from the passenger area. The V-drive connects the engine to the propeller with a V-shaped driveshaft. With this angled drive shaft, the engine is in the stern.

This gives two benefits: closer contact with passengers and a relatively small wake. "The V-drive opens up the cockpit area" while it still "offers water-skiers a small and easy wake, because it still utilizes the flat bottom" of inboard boats, reported *Trailer Boats* magazine. The Super Sport has intimate wraparound seating that gives passengers "a feeling of being at home in the living room. Passengers sit closer and talk more easily, without shouting around a motorbox in their midst," the magazine's reporter added.[6]

The Super Sport may attract more families with the extra room; like the Sport, it's eighteen inches longer than the Ski Nautique. The Super Sport's wake is fine for wakeboarding, tubing, and recreational skiing, though not as smooth as in the traditional Ski Nautique, the preferred boat for tournament and show skiing.

WHAT THE OWNERS SAY

Correct Craft customers responding to a one-year owners' survey seem very satisfied with their boats and the company. Customer satisfaction in 1996 was 97 percent, and 98 percent of the respondents would recommend the boat to a friend. The top reasons for purchasing the boat were product quality and performance, mentioned by 82 percent and 73 percent, respectively. And contrary to some rivals' claims, few buyers are professional skiers wanting an expensive boat. The typical buyer uses a Nautique for recreational skiing; only 16 percent use the boats for practice or actual tournament competition.[7]

Customers often put their appreciation in writing. Steven Horwood of Michigan wrote that "my wife, Laura, and I love our 1993 Ski Nautique. . . . We both grew up in boating families, and it was only natural that we too would buy a boat after we were married." Horwood described their search for "the perfect inboard ski boat" as they compared "every inboard on the market." He concluded that "the quality and craftsmanship that I saw in your boats was truly top notch, not to mention the styling, which also sets it apart from the rest."

Two years after the purchase, the Horwoods had their first child, and Steven ended the letter by describing Laura and himself: "We are proud parents of a wonderful little girl and proud owners of a Ski Nautique."[8]

A pilot for Delta Air Lines bought his first Ski Nautique after forty-five years of driving and skiing in other boats. "In my first forty-five years of boat driving and waterskiing, I have always felt I had to apologize for my lack of power to properly get big skiers up on a single ski," Victor Wadsley wrote. "In my forty-sixth year, I just sit back and smile." Calling his Nautique "an incredible boat . . . a marvel and a wonder," Wadsley concludes his letter: "Put your trust in God, a good airplane, and a sound boat!"[9]

Correct Craft management appreciates its customers, too. Beginning in 1994, the company has had annual reunions of owners at all four Sea World theme parks. It is the premier activity of NOA (pronounced "Noah"), the Nautique Owners Association. W. N., who rides a Harley-Davidson motorcycle, credits fellow biker Paul Williams with the name NOA. Harley riders belong to HOG (Harley Owners Group), but Correct Craft management knew the acrostic NOA fit the boat company well. "NOA has a biblical tone, even though it's not spelled the same," says Larry Meddock, marketing vice president. The company's slogan is "On the waters of the world since 1925." Noah, perhaps the world's first boatbuilder, lived on the waters of the world for one hundred and fifty days. It seemed the perfect match.

Loyal Correct Craft owners who join NOA receive a Nautique hat, T-shirt, decal, and membership card, as well as information on national and local events with other boat owners. The highlight is the annual reunion at Sea World, where owners display their boats, compete for prizes, swap information, have a fun time at the park, and even sell or trade boat and ski equipment. The reunions include a lunch, cap, and admission to Sea World, all for a nominal registration fee ($5.00 in 1996). In 1996, 4,700 Nautique owners attended the four reunions, and they displayed more than 400 boats.

TEAM SPONSORSHIPS

Correct Craft pioneered the concept of team sponsorship when it introduced its first Ski Nautique in 1961, and today its Team Nautique promotional staff includes some of the biggest names in pro skiing. Among the 1996 team members were Helena Kiellander, a three-time world slalom champion; Kristi Overton Johnson, the woman's slalom record holder; Andy Mapple, the men's slalom record holder; Bruce Neville, world record holder in distance jumping and a world-class three-event skier; and Ron Scarpa, the most decorated barefoot skier ever, winner of dozens of tournaments.

They and other Team Nautique members practice exclusively with Correct Craft Nautiques, and many rave about its ride and wake characteristics.

The company receives a few letters each month from athletes wanting to join the team. In a sport in which skiers have promotional agreements with makers of water skis, towropes, and even sunglasses, the athletes want to land an agreement with a quality boat company. So Correct Craft can pick and choose the members of its team.

INBOARD VERSUS OUTBOARD

Company officials hope that demand for its inboard-engine boats will increase as prospective customers become more aware of the inboard's advantages. Inboard ski boats are a small segment of the recreational boating market—about 6 percent. Most buyers prefer the outboard ski boat or a larger inboard/outboard (I/O) pleasure craft.

One reason for the lower sales of inboard boats is cost, as inboards carry a higher price tag and offer performance engines by Ford and General Motors. (The Ski Nautique features Ford engines by PleasureCraft, with an optional GM engine available.) Another reason is image: Many potential buyers regard the slimmer, compact inboard craft as too snug and less relaxing than an outboard boat. But with its open bow seating, up to nine people can enjoy cruising in a Ski Nautique, as well as in the open bow Super Sport Nautique with its wrap-around front seating. "We hope families will see these are fun, roomy boats," Scott Mohr says. "With the ability of the hulls to smooth the path, it's a smooth, safe ride, too." The company wants to convince boat enthusiasts that Nautiques have room to let family and friends stretch out.

Most people who buy a ski boat keep it five to seven years before replacing it. Correct Craft and other inboard boat makers hope to educate boat owners to the value advantage of starting with an inboard. Nautique owners are "typically third boat buyers who are stepping up from the I/O," according to Meddock.

The compromise recreational boat is the I/O combination, which offers an internal engine that has good power and is not exposed to the water. However, most of its drive mechanism is underwater, and the engine expends much of its power turning spines, cogs, and gears. The sophisticated outdrive system must "turn driveshafts twice at ninety-degree angles," resulting in an energy loss, according to Meddock. The lost energy and efficiency and extra wear on the moving parts underwater soon add up to needed repairs. "The drive is going to break or corrode," Meddock says. Such an occurrence is unlikely with an inboard boat.

In addition, the inboard-engine driver no longer worries about loss of horizon, and he gets improved throttle response and better wake for the skier in the back as well. Loss of horizon occurs during the initial acceleration, when the throttle opens and the bow rises into the air. With the I/O weight more toward the back (stern), the driver loses sight of the horizon for the first few seconds before the boat's front settles down onto the surface. With outboard engines, greater RPMs (revolutions per second) are needed to generate greater horsepower.

The reason is that outboards are two-cycle engines, which develop torque more slowly than the inboard's four-cycle engine and need more horsepower to move the boat through the water.

"What that means to you as a boater is that your real throttle response doesn't happen until the final one inch on your throttle," Meddock says. "That's where all the juice is. Let's say I weigh 200 pounds and you're trying to give me a decent ski ride, and I want to be pulled 36 miles per hour. I've spent all day giving everybody—the kids, my friends, my wife's friends —a ski ride. Now it's my turn to water-ski. I ask my wife to take over. My wife is trying to hang onto this beast, trying to peak its optimum RPM range. She's trying to hold the speed. And I'm screaming at her, 'C'mon, can't you hold it?' We're yelling at each other. What fun is that?"

"For those who have been there," with the limits of the outboard and I/O, Meddock concludes, the inboard's response is appealing. The Nautique, for instance, gives an exact, lineal throttle response: Move the throttle forward one-eighth of an inch and the speed will increase proportionately. With its inboard engine, the Nautique does not lose horizon, moving straight ahead during the initial acceleration. "And it tracks like it's on a rail," Meddock says.

Other positive features of the inboard are its driving response—what's called its driveability—and its towing features, or "skiability." "You can steer the inboard with your fingertip, whereas with an I/O or an outboard you must muscle it with two hands," Meddock explains, "because you have this 'foot' in the water with all this torque on it. Without that torque, it's like you have power steering. You can talk to each other in the cockpit because there's no noise." And the wake is minimal because of the engine's more centered position.

With its roomier, quieter, and better-built boats, Correct Craft hopes to continue catching the wave among recreational boaters in the coming years.

Notes

1. Jim Youngs, "Towing the Line," *Popular Mechanics,* July 1994, 53. For 1987 test results, see Frank Sargeant, "Ski Boat Shootout," *Popular Mechanics,* November 1987, 86–90.
2. Robert Stephens, "Evolution and Revolution," *Water Ski,* February 1995, 50.
3. At the same record-setting tournament with the '97 Ski Nautique, Kristi skied around 5 and then 6 buoys at 39 1/2 feet off before moving to 41 off.
4. Zenon Bilas, "Skiing Is Believing," *Trailer Boats,* July 1996, 185–86.
5. Rob May, "Xtreme Xposure," *Water Ski,* September/October 1996, 6.
6. Zenon Bilas, "Serious Skiboats," *Trailer Boats,* February 1996, 66.
7. The results came from 569 owners of Correct Craft boats who purchased a '95 model.
8. "Feedback," *Nautique News,* spring/ summer 1996, 12.
9. Ibid., 1.

Chapter 12
On the Waters of Sea World

everal prospectors, panning for gold in northern California, strike it rich in 1849. As retold at four Sea
World theme parks, the old story is loaded with action
and humor for the 1990s crowd. It also has a novel twist sure to
please: Most of the actors enter or exit—and often perform—
on water skis.

The skiing begins after the prospectors start celebrating at
dockside. A boat pulling a half-dozen women skiers, including
some of the prospectors' wives, drives up to the beach. And
soon trick skiers are everywhere. The show has triple forward
jumps, one-ski entrances, barefoot skiing and landings, and an
almost-collision of boats.

The humor is witty and knowing. As the men watch the
girls land, they decide to "tidy up." They shed their dirty
prospecting duds for fancy suits to court the women. Eventually
the men settle down, with wives and wealth, to the town's new
neighborhood: Gold Bullion Estates. During their quest for
riches and romance, the ten male prospectors (all of whom
happen to be talented skiers) fall into dunking ponds, dance
with the audience, and make some great ski maneuvers in the
large lake just offshore, often with the women they're after.

Like most good ski shows, the "Gold Rush Ski Show" ends

with a pyramid of skiers—fourteen, with the women riding the men's shoulders in the three-level formation. And like all ski shows at Sea World, the skiers are pulled by Ski Nautiques by Correct Craft. It's been that way since 1986, and their contract will keep Ski Nautique pulling Sea World skiers at least through December 1999. "I don't have any reason to think we won't be with Correct Craft after that, too," says Art Freedman, vice president of entertainment at Sea World of Florida.

The shows have changed over the years. Before the Gold Rush show, skiers spoofed beach parties, surfing, and cool hamburger hangouts in "Beach Blanket Ski Party." Prior to that, ski performers battled as the Hatfields and McCoys, complete with tin lizzies, floating houseboats, and diving revenue agents escaping wild gunshots. In 1996, Sea World kept the spectators coming back with "Baywatch at Sea World," a takeoff on the syndicated TV show featuring lifeguards, sunbathers, swimmers, and a supposed drowning victim. With numerous rescues —just like the TV show—the show climaxes when someone on the beach accidentally activates an old torpedo, sending it speeding toward the center of the lake, where it explodes in a cascade of fireworks.

THE EXCLUSIVE TOWBOAT AT SEA WORLD

Three Ski Nautiques pull the skiers through the action. Since there are Sea World marine parks in four states, that's twelve Ski Nautiques strutting their stuff. Correct Craft hasn't always been the official towboat at Sea World, however. Years ago, Mercury Outboards had the job. When Mercury could no longer supply boats in exchange for promotional considerations, Sea World asked the inboard boat makers to offer bids. Correct Craft's was chosen.

When its contract agreement was expiring in 1994, Correct Craft and another industry leader made competitive bids. "The [second inboard manufacturer] offered some cash," Freedman revealed, indicating the offer was slightly superior to that of Correct Craft. "But we feel Correct Craft is a better product. We have a long relationship with them. And relationship counts more than money.

"Our drivers have driven both boats in tournaments and prefer Correct Craft. We assume the quality will continue. We received very good service" during earlier contracts, Freedman adds, explaining why Sea Worlds in Cleveland, San Antonio, San Diego, and his own Orlando park agreed to accept the Correct Craft offer.

It's a typical promotional arrangement. Correct Craft supplies the boats and free service, along with water skis and assorted skiing accessories. In exchange, the name *Ski Nautique* is displayed prominently on the sides of the boats, where spectators can't miss seeing it. Every six months, Correct Craft provides new boats. That's not because the old boats are suffering from wear and tear. Rather, as almost-new boats, they're in great demand with boaters, and Correct Craft can recoup some of the cost by selling them.

The boats prove their worth every year in Sea World's laboratory of quick starts, stops, fast turns, and steady speeds for the ski performers. In an average year, skiers perform two or three shows most days, but they do up to five during the summers to accommodate the vacation crowds. And while the skiers may change at times, the boats go show after show after show. In 1994, for example, Correct Craft boats were driven 304,467 nautical miles during 662,415 shows at the four parks. The drivers and skiers put the boats through their paces, with 420 engine shifts per show and more than 10 million engine shifts per year.

Sea World officials are loud in their praise for the Nautique line. "The Nautiques are definitely the strongest boat we've ever used in terms of maneuverability, power, and safety," declares Dan Stewart, Sea World of Texas production manager. "From my exposure to a wide variety of ski boats," adds former entertainment director Jim Timon of Sea World's California park, "the Correct Craft Ski Nautique is by far, hands down, the best there is. You wouldn't believe what these boats go through. The Correct Craft's never given us a moment of worry."

PRAISE FROM DRIVERS AND SKIERS

One senior driver at the Orlando park says drivers love Nautiques for the reliable ride they offer: "Nautiques are highly predictable. Because of the small space that we're driving them in, by the time you start, it's time to stop," says Barry Diesel. "Most importantly, the Nautiques handle equally well in both directions—whereas other inboards tend to slide."[1]

The strongest endorsements come from the skiers themselves, who ride behind Nautiques every day. During the 1980s and 1990s, Terri Garner performed eleven years at the Florida Sea World. She was so impressed with the product that she bought one herself, a 1989 Ski Nautique. "As an owner," she says, "I'd rather pay more and have something that is good quality, reliable, and the best-driving boat to ski behind."

She was pleased to learn that the boat, which she bought used, has kept its value. The same year she bought her Nautique, her husband, Kent, and she purchased a Toyota automobile. Five years later they sold the car, which had depreciated more than 50 percent, a normal rate. The boat, however, had kept its value. "It did not depreciate one penny" from the purchase price, Terri reports.

Terri became the ski show director in Orlando and continued to perform through 1995. She is now ski show manager and director, leading forty performers. In any one show, twenty-two team members appear, including seventeen skiers, two high divers, and three boat drivers. She urged her boss, Art Freedman, to stay with Correct Craft when it was time to negotiate a new contract. And she tells her friends not to settle for a less-expensive boat, which, she says, depreciates more and is of lower quality.

"People who want the best quality [typically] buy Correct Craft," Terri explains. "Some people may not know the difference," but, she says, the materials and handling characteristics of the boat make it the best. "In the way they drive, in the way they ride, there's no comparison in my mind."

In its temperate climate, the Orlando Sea World ski show goes on year-round, making it a great place for show skiers seeking a career with steady income, a chance to stay in shape, and the opportunity to develop a family of close friends. As program director, Terri receives résumés and inquiries almost weekly. The average age of the skiers—twenty-seven—is older than at the other parks, showing the maturity and limited turnover among the team members.

The Sea World performers have a reputation of being a diverse yet unified crew: They come from all over, including representatives from Oregon, North Dakota, and Wisconsin. Only five are from Florida. They also have a reputation as being a gathering point for caring Christians. A few who joined the Florida ski show later told Terri, "Before I came here, I heard there were a lot of Christians."

Several women skiers participate in home fellowship groups and leadership Bible studies. Terri says women "have met the Lord" through such Bible studies and the sensitive witness of teammates. Nine men attended Bible studies in 1996, looking at a men's issues book from Promise Keepers, the national men's movement that emphasizes spiritual growth through accountability, attending church, and supporting one's family. Over the years, male members have often gathered for prayer breakfasts and Bible studies at homes after practices.

PRO SKIERS, SHOW SKIERS, AND CHRISTIANITY

Today, about 25 percent of the team are Christians, Terri estimates. That percentage reflects the influence of Christians in the ranks of both competitive and show skiers.

Seven championship skiers were featured in a 1985 video, *Living Waters,* talking about their Christian faith and showing their stuff behind the towboat, including three-time international water-ski jump champion Harold Cole and former barefoot national champions Mike Botti and Lori Powell. No new highlights video of Christian champions has been made in the '90s, but the ten-minute video, with plenty of trick and jump skiing set to music, is still being shown around the world.

One German skier visiting the United States took the video back to Frankfurt. One night he told people in a tavern, "How would you like to see some hot skiing?" The customers said yes, the skier popped in the tape, and soon there were cheers and whistles—and the patrons heard the gospel. *Living Waters* still is often shown at camps, youth meetings, and even ski schools.

Two of the Orlando Sea World performers, Botti and Andy Hansen, have been active in a water-ski affiliate of the Fellowship of Christian Athletes. Andy is now owner and an instructor at the Benzel Ski School in Groveland, Florida. Before he became a Christian, he loved to party, drink beer, and impress "the prettiest, most popular girls." After two serious automobile accidents, a near drowning under a platform at Sea World, and falling almost 300 feet when his delta wing kite collapsed, Andy began to get serious about life.

The four close calls with death, Andy says, were how "God really started to get my attention." He became a Christian after a fellow skier, Sherry McNarry, invited him to a Bible study. He started attending regularly and learned "what it means to have a personal relationship with Jesus Christ." The study leader made it clear that God "gave us the gift of His Son, and through belief in Him we could be saved. There was nothing we could do on our own but to open our hearts and let Christ come in."

After Andy became a Christian, he and other skiers held Bible studies for Sea World skiers and others; a friend began one for Cypress Gardens skiers as well. Andy believes the number of Christians in show waterskiing is not unusually high, but that Christian skiers tend to be vibrant in their faith and concerned for other performers' spiritual and physical needs.

Non-Christian skiers who come to Sea World of Florida find the Christian skiers friendly and sensitive. Some do not join the Christians for Bible studies, while others do. For Jacqueline Reece of Houston, a fifteen-year skiing veteran, including four in Orlando, she found herself intrigued by the faith of her team-mates. After she graduated from the University of Texas, she came to Sea World of Florida to train for the 1988 opening of Sea World in San Antonio.

At five feet, seven inches, Jacqueline is taller than most women skiers, who typically are petite yet strong. In show ski-ing, there are more lifts than in competition skiing. Women climb to the tops of pyramids; men hoist them on their shoul-ders in double lifts. As in gymnastics, strong yet small women are ideal.

But Jacqueline's talent won out over size concerns, so she came to Florida for three weeks of training. Physically, she looked down on her trainer, who was exactly five feet tall. But Jacqueline otherwise was impressed with Pattie Weber. She appreciated Pattie's friendly demeanor. Her trainer even showed her some of the Orlando sights. And on Jacqueline's final day in Florida, before she would return to Texas and pre-pare for the new Sea World opening, Pattie invited her to church. Jacqueline said yes, partly out of feeling obligated, but also because of a deep curiosity.

"While in college, I had been searching," she says. "I had a meeting with a Campus Crusade for Christ person and talked with her. And Pattie talked about the Lord a lot and read her Bible. So I was curious."

That morning at Calvary Assembly in Orlando, Jacqueline made Pattie's faith her own. She accepted Jesus as her Savior.

"It was like someone turned the light on in my life," she reports. "I listened to the pastor, and it felt like he was talking to me that day." She doesn't remember the topic, but she remembers how he ended the message: "If you have been touched by what has been said here, then come forward. We'd like to pray with you. Make a commitment to Jesus right now." Jacqueline hesitated a moment, and then she walked to the front.

"I realized this was it—this was my moment to come to God."

Afterward, before she boarded her plane, Pattie gave her a Bible and "wrote the date—the date I accepted Christ—inside," Jacqueline says. She still has that Bible.

In February 1988, Pattie followed Jacqueline to San Antonio to become a lead trainer for the ski team as it prepared for the inaugural season. Pattie stayed seven months, putting the entire team through its paces and discipling Jacqueline in the Christian life. The grand opening in May went smoothly, and Pattie performed several star tricks for the first show.

Pattie returned to Orlando at the end of summer, and five years later Jacqueline joined the Florida team. The two have become close friends.

A LOW-KEY APPROACH

The Christian climate in the Orlando team is low key, Terri notes. "It amazes me that everybody here knows who the Christians are," she says. "When someone has a problem, even if he or she is not a Christian, the people whose help is sought are the Christians. It's almost as if the person knows that's the direction he should be going in. But it's not until you have problems that you go that way."

Terri says that low-key approach helped her find Christ as well. When she joined the Sea World ski team, she assumed she *was* a Christian. "I believed in God, and I believed in the Bible. But I didn't know what the Bible said. I had never taken the time to really know about Jesus." In the company of loving Christians, though, Terri began to realize her need. Several gave her audio tapes of messages. They were sensitive and caring, Terri says, not pushy. She began attending an Orlando church. Meanwhile her husband, a fellow skier, was a nominal Christian who watched her journey to faith. He realized his need for a fresh commitment to Christ as well.

"It was such a blessing—both of us at the same time went in the same direction." Kent and Terri Garner now have two daughters, and in 1996 the Garner family took the summer off to help at a Christian camp in Colorado, teaching skiing and running the camp store.

When Terri finally became a Christian, she wondered, *Okay, now what do I do?* She explains, "I felt my life was supposed to totally change, but I didn't know what to do. But it's amazing; all you have to do is trust in Him. The Lord will take care of everything else." The several women skiers who were Christians were ready to talk and listen. Watching them, studying the Bible—which now began to make a lot of sense—she started to be convicted about "little things that were not right anymore." As she notes, "The Lord will show you the way. He takes the blinders off."

At Sea World, many of the show skiers have clear vision, living for God. And Ski Nautiques, speeding on the waters of Sea World, pull the performers steadily and faithfully through their routines, to the delight of spectators and skiers alike.

Note

1. "Show Business," *Nautique News,* spring 1993, 19.

Chapter 13

A Firm Witness

*A*s a location manager working for Disney, Universal, and other movie companies, Larry Meddock liked scouting out venues and securing clearances. As an above-average water-skier, he also liked jumping more than 100 feet and had even helped a San Diego water-ski company sell skis, binders, and wet suits before turning to the movies. He knew about Ski Nautiques from the San Diego connection and had even used five of the boats for several scenes in the Disney movie *Freaky Friday.* But saying good-bye to temperamental directors for wake-smoothing towboats was not something he had ever considered.

He first met Correct Craft's then-president W. O. Meloon during an afternoon break at a national sales conference in Florida. "I was a fan of their boats," he says. He took the afternoon off to see their headquarters, told W. O. about his respect for Correct Craft, and even agreed to sell Correct Craft boats in California later that year during post-production on a film (a four-month period). But leaving the fast pace of Hollywood for the wide-open spaces of Orlando had little appeal. Eventually, though, W. O.'s compassion and persistence would pay off for a man who, deep down, was unsettled in his spirit.

Larry agreed to visit W. O. for a job interview at Meloon's

request, but he came out of respect more than an itching for a change. His wife, Jan, and he stayed a week, looked, and talked. "At the end, we sat down, and Walt offered me a job," Larry says. "He told me what he was going to pay me. I said, 'Thanks, but no thanks.'" The offer, though good by Florida and boat-industry standards, could not compete with what the motion picture industry paid. He was earning four times the salary Correct Craft proposed. The Meddocks returned to Southern California.

But W. O. persisted. Every couple of months, he would call Larry in Los Angeles. The calls were courteous but short, as W. O. inquired about Larry's interest and Larry kindly declined. The third time, Larry felt it was time to clarify his feelings and W. O.'s motives. After the friendly greeting, Larry told the president, "Mr. Meloon, if you're forcing me to make a decision, I have to say no."

"Larry, I'm not forcing you to make a decision," W. O. replied. "You're not filling a vacant position. So whenever you're ready, the position will be ready for you, because we just want you."

"Okay, thank you."

AN UNEASY FEELING

But this time as he hung up the phone, Larry began to have second thoughts. It was a sunny June day in California, and he was beginning a new movie project, yet he felt uneasy.

"I was being consumed by the whole Hollywood scene," he says. "Everything you ever heard about Hollywood is true— the drugs, the alcohol, the women—everything. I could see myself going right down that path." Though Larry had not been pulled into any of those practices, he sensed the temptation would be hard to resist with a marriage that "was going the wrong way," he recalls. "We're human. It takes a real special person to keep saying no to the parties and that atmosphere. There are many opportunities to trip up." Often Meddock was being whisked to meetings in limousines and flown around in jets. In this environment, he was seeing less of his wife, yet he hardly missed the decreased time at home with his family.

"There was always a party at the end of the shooting," he continues. "You're hanging out with the beautiful people. I was finding excuses not to come home. Instead of being home at six o'clock, I'd roll home at nine o'clock. Then I'd start rolling in at ten o'clock. It didn't take a rocket scientist to figure it out. I began asking myself, *Larry, what are you doing here, pal? Which way are you going? You've got to make a decision real soon.*"

Five months later, Larry was on Venice Beach, working on another movie. He felt tension with the film company and with himself, and looking at the blue Pacific Ocean couldn't calm him. During the film shoot, he received still another phone call from Orlando.

It was W. O. Meloon. "Are you ready to come to work yet?" he asked.

Larry couldn't give an immediate answer, though he admitted he had more interest now.

Several months later, the lies and frantic pace of Hollywood came to a head. He had received clearance to use a street corner in Venice, California, for a movie stunt. The film director had told Meddock he planned to drop a twenty-seven-foot cabin cruiser on a Volkswagen. The boat's tanks would be removed, the director promised. They would use only a corner of the block, and there was no need to close the street to traffic. On that basis, city police had issued a permit.

But when the director said, "Action!" technicians dropped a cabin cruiser filled with 200 gallons of gas in the middle of the street. The director's lies resulted in a scene out of a Keystone Cops comedy. The firefighters yelled at Meddock as they cleaned up the hazardous fuel. The police were after the director for forcing them to close a full city block and reroute traffic. And the local Taco Bell manager yelled at Meddock for the unending line of cars winding through his parking lot due to the detour. Most drivers were angry at the delay, and none ordered from the drive-through.

By the end of the day, as he was driving home, Meddock

stopped at a car wash in the beach community and found a pay phone. He called Correct Craft, and after exchanging greetings with the president, he came to the point: "If you'll have me, I'd like to come to work for you."

"Amen. Come on," W. O. said. "Praise the Lord, I've prayed for this phone call."

When he returned to Correct Craft for a final interview, Larry spent extended time with Walt N., then general manager, and learned about trusting in the Meloon word.

"Larry, I don't know what we're going to do with you," W. N. said. "But trust me; if you come, you'll never regret it."

The two had met only briefly during Meddock's earlier visit. The Hollywood location manager was impressed by the general manager's sincerity and commitment. "I thought that was pretty significant," Larry says. "The guy didn't know me, and I didn't know him. But he said, 'Trust me; you'll never regret it.' And I never have."

His wife was less convinced, knowing the family income would drop and that she and their two daughters would pull up roots in Anaheim and move 2,500 miles. They knew no one in Orlando. Larry waited, hoping his wife would agree to the career change.

"There were a lot of tears and uncertainty," Larry recalls. The two had several conversations as he tried to explain his motive. Jan realized her husband wanted to improve their marriage, escaping the Hollywood scene. She saw the sacrifices and risks he would make in taking a new job. So she finally said yes.

"I have a special lady," Larry declares about his partner of more than twenty-five years. The relocation to Florida, though an adjustment, solidified their marriage, with regular working hours, a more leisurely pace, and the southern hospitality. The warm, family atmosphere at work was a welcome change from the party life of Hollywood that had ripped at the Meddocks' marriage and at Larry's soul.

"GOD, YOU HAVE MY ATTENTION"

A few years later, on an unusually cold Orlando morning when the thermometer read 25 degrees, Larry Meddock drove to watch a friend fly model airplanes. Larry's two older daughters were with him, but Jan stayed home to watch their ten-month-old.

As he drove, a nineteen-year-old girl high on drugs ran a stop sign and struck the Meddock station wagon. No one was wearing seat belts, and Larry was thrown out the driver's door. His four-year-old daughter, Kristen, was unhurt in the backseat. But Casey, three, went through the windshield. Mom had dressed her in a leather snowsuit and a stocking cap pulled down to her eyebrows. Casey suffered a concussion and lots of superficial facial cuts. The leather coat shredded as she slid down the street, but it protected most of her body.

Larry says now, "I remember lying in the gutter and saying, 'God, You now have my attention. God, give me a second chance.'" A couple months later, Larry joined Ralph Meloon at a banquet sponsored by the Christian Businessmen's Committee, and the father of three and former Hollywood location manager received Christ as his Savior.

The Meloons' Christian faith was not the main factor that led him to become a follower of Christ. The accident was, and he's grateful for a full recovery for Casey and himself. But the Meloons' faith has helped him to trust God more and see the need to consult God daily.

"I enjoy watching them reflecting the Word and trying to do what's right," he explains. "I know they do that. In their struggles, they always try to do what's right." He noted one day that he quoted Scripture in a memo he sent to employees. "If someone had told me twenty years ago when I made a movie that I could have made my point quoting Scripture, I would have said, 'You're nuts!' But here the Meloons have taught me there's an answer for everything if I refer to the Word. The Meloons have taught me, 'Larry, that Bible is there for a reason. It can help you with every aspect of your life.'

"As they have gotten into tough situations and shared with me, I've learned the process of the Christian life. They have never come in here and preached to me, judged me, or scolded me."

AN INTEREST IN THE
WORKERS' SPIRITUAL WELFARE

The Meloons' strong faith not only affects corporate policy, but it also motivates their interest in the spiritual welfare of Correct Craft's workers. For many years, the company held monthly chapel meetings featuring Christian films or guest speakers. Those meetings are now quarterly, as schedules and locations make it difficult to assemble everyone once a month. Speakers have ranged from sports stars like basketball's Pete Maravich and Meadowlark Lemon and football's Rosey Grier and Bobby Bowden (coach of the national champion Florida State Seminoles) to Christian leaders like Charles Colson and Billy Graham.

The chapel program dates back to 1943, and Graham spoke in 1951, when more than 1,000 visitors overflowed the plant. A few years later, the Graham evangelistic team held one week of meetings at the plant, and several spiritual decisions were made.

W. O. and Billy Graham are friends from the 1940s, when Orlando businessman Don Mott, active in the Christian Businessmen's Committee and Youth for Christ, introduced Meloon to Graham, then a YFC vice president and traveling evangelist. In fact, Billy Graham and his new bride, Ruth, had their first Thanksgiving meal as a married couple with W. O. and his wife, Ann, and the Motts. Graham knows about the Meloons' principles and Christian witness, and he says of W. O., "Walt and his family have been close personal friends since the early days of my ministry. Walt is one of God's choice servants in the business world."[1]

Attendance at chapel is optional. Those who don't attend are still paid as the plant closes for one hour. "It's a great witness," says design/engineering manager Bill Snook, who appreciates the company's sensitivity to its workers. How do the workers like it? "Most like to go," says Marty Mitchell, a receptionist for twenty years. "They get to sit down. It's refreshing. I don't know everyone's motives. But the plan of salvation is given."

When and how a Christian business leader should present spiritual ideas in the workplace concerns most Christian executives, according to Laura Nash, adjunct professor at the Boston University School of Management. In her book *Believers in Business,* she surveyed eighty-five chief executive officers (CEOs) and found seven tensions involving faith and work. The tensions ranged from the love for God versus the quest for profit to how to be a faithful witness in the secular setting of work.[2] Nash, who is a former member of the Harvard Business School faculty, found that CEOs bear witness to their faith in one of three ways: overt institutional witness, overt personal witness, and indirect witness.[3] At Correct Craft, the Meloons practice all three.

The institutional witness includes Scripture verses in product catalogs and inspirational stories in the company magazine, *Nautique News,* both of which are distributed to the public. The 1995 catalog, for instance, had a two-page spread showing a couple driving a Nautique Super Sport across a lake on a sunny day. In the upper left corner of the photo are the only words, the lines from a Scripture verse: "O! Give thanks unto the LORD, for HE is good, for HIS love endures FOREVER. Psalm 107:1."

The 1997 catalogs, one for each of the four Nautique models, have their own Scripture verses above a greeting from W. N. For boaters who don't always think about the spiritual issues of life, it probably catches their attention, and they become aware of Correct Craft's priorities as they read: "'Love the Lord your God with all your heart and with all your soul and with all your might.' Deuteronomy 6:5" (NASB, in the Sport Nautique catalog); or "'May the God of hope fill you with all joy and peace as you trust in him, so that you may overflow with hope by the power of the Holy Spirit.' Romans 15:13" (NIV, in the Ski Nautique 176 catalog).

NOT A HARD SELL

As Larry Meddock appreciates that the company does not "preach at" or "scold" its employees with its Christianity, Bill Snook appreciates the Meloons' sensitivity to its workers and the public. "They don't take a hard-sell position," he says. "The literature says, 'We are Christians, and we honor the Lord in the things we do. We're telling you that. We're not preaching at you.'" The company magazine always contains an inspirational article, either a ministry a worker participates in or a thought derived from the Bible.

"What we try to do is make a simple, straightforward, nonoffensive testimony to the fact that we are different," W. N. explains. "And the minute people think you're different, they start asking questions about what, who, when, where, and all the rest of it. Opportunities begin to open for a Christian testimony. One does not have to be aggressive in presenting the gospel."

W. N. admits he hesitated about adding Scripture to the catalog. "At first I was very uncomfortable about putting the Scripture in the catalog, but I did it out of respect for my father and my uncle and my grandfather. I didn't believe in it, but I accepted it. And in doing so, I honored all three of them. I have now become very comfortable with it. The Scripture teaches that you will honor your elders. . . . So there's a lot of reasons for doing those things. Life is a lot easier when you obey the Scripture."

The company has received scattered criticism from customers who are uncomfortable with the inspirational stories and the gospel message in *Nautique News.* Several have asked to be taken off the mailing list, "but a lot more have thanked us for it," says Ralph Meloon. According to W. O., "We get letters from people who say, 'We're happy there's a Christian outfit we can do business with. We bought the boat because you are Christians.'"

"Thank you for operating a business based on Christian principles and being up-front about it in your public statements and actions," wrote Wallace and Betty Skage of Lancaster, California.[4]

Responding to the smattering of criticism, including that of a few dealers who left the company over its strong Christian witness, W. N. says concerning the use of Scripture in the catalog, "I don't think we would want to—or dare to—drop it." It's a matter of obeying Christ's call to be witnesses, he argues. "You either believe God or you don't. We're here as witnesses, and when we aren't a witness any longer, we are hardly here for anything."

Many of the CEOs in Nash's study engage in personal witness because they feel their large company must relate to the culture. Often this witness is in response to inquiries, for CEOs, aware of their power and authority, do not want to unduly influence workers. Many keep a Bible on their desk or have a religious symbol nearby, ready to talk about their faith when asked.

For instance, when an employee comes in to explain a serious health problem, the boss could say, "I'll certainly pray about it." That's the approach of Ed Yates, then CEO of Highland Park Cafeterias, who notes, "I could have said 'I think you should become a Christian.' But saying 'I'll pray for you' said something about my belief without infringing on her privacy. Maybe she will be interested in asking me about it. Maybe not."[5]

That approach, of compassion for their workers and a deep yearning that employees find spiritual peace, typifies the Meloons, according to their staff. Meddock has seen it in W. O., who has stopped by Meddock's office just to chat. Snook has seen it in the words of W. N. And all employees see it in the presence of Harold Meloon, the third Meloon brother and the company chaplain.

THE HEART OF A CHAPLAIN

As chaplain, Harold prays with workers who have health and family problems, and he visits those in the hospital. Harold has been chaplain since 1973, and he has seen many results over the years. He remembers "Fred," who worked in the trailer division (now closed) and had a heart condition. Fred was only a couple years older than Harold, and the two became friends.

One evening after work, Harold presented the gospel to Fred and another worker. Harold reports, "I told them, 'Right tonight, if you make a decision for Jesus Christ, and say by stepping over this line in the concrete that you have made that decision in your heart, He will save you.'

"They both turned me down."

But later, when Fred was hospitalized, he welcomed Harold's visit. "He informed me that he had 'stepped over the line.' I knew immediately what he was talking about. He was just glowing as he told me that."

Fred lived a few more years, "enough for me to know there had been a definite change in his life," Harold says. And he worked a little longer at Correct Craft before retiring. Back on the job, Fred told several other employees, "I wish I had made the decision to follow Christ much sooner."

"I had the privilege of preaching at his funeral," Harold concludes.

Harold operated his own business, Southern Metal Fabricating Company, for more than twenty years. There he and his workers built playground equipment for parks and schools, and boat trailers for Correct Craft. Later he sold the property to Correct Craft. Now in his middle seventies, Harold is grateful the company remains committed to Christian principles.

"First, I'm grateful they do take a stand," he says. "They give me opportunities to talk to the employees about spiritual things. It's not a closed situation. We have these quarterly chapel meetings and give the employees time to come to them." Harold helps organize those meetings.

"BOMBARDED WITH CHRISTIANS"

Some employees have heard the gospel on the job through interested coworkers. Shortly after joining Correct Craft, engineer Bill Snook says, "God started bombarding my wife and me with other Christians." The Snooks had been attending a church in Sebring but felt like visitors there. But outside the church, he met several Christians who shared their faith. His landlord, Rick Jones, was a former member of the Sea World ski team and a committed Christian. Bill was amazed. "I just went through the newspaper and picked houses, and he becomes my landlord." Then he met the Correct Craft receptionist, Marty Mitchell, who listened closely and asked about his family.

"I met happy, vibrant people," he says. "They weren't preaching at me, saying, 'You're living in sin.' Instead, they showed me the abundant life. Even in the midst of the trials she was going through, Marty still had a joy. I had never encountered that kind of Christian."

Next he met a Bible student at a lake where he skied. Dennis Rosenquist, a former competition skier, introduced himself and eventually explained his Christian faith. Months later, the now curious engineer asked Marty to recommend a good church. She suggested two churches that believe and teach the Scriptures. "That's what's important," Marty said. "Find a church where the Bible is preached."

Bill decided to visit the second church, the one Marty herself attended. When he asked for directions, he learned it was less than a five-minute drive from home. He hesitated and didn't go for a couple weeks after he learned 5,000 people attend Calvary Assembly; the Snooks had always been in small churches.

But two weeks later, the Snooks strolled onto the huge church "campus," their four-year-old, John, in tow. John was cranky, and Bill felt lost. He couldn't locate Marty, as he had hoped, and wasn't sure where to go. Then he saw a familiar face. Rick Jones was walking up to them, a big grin on his face. This was his church, too. Rick escorted them to the toddlers' room to drop off John, and then he led them to the church foyer. Smiling faces and handshakes greeted them, and in the background, he could hear a woman vocalist/pianist singing quietly.

"We ended up sitting in the balcony," Bill says. "I don't remember what the pastor preached on. But that day I met the Lord. And so did my wife."

He gives some credit to the Meloons for preparing his heart to respond to the Christian message. He had been working at the firm less than a year when he visited Calvary, and he still remembered his final job interview with the president, when W. N. explained that the company was owned and operated by Christians: "We don't require that you be a Christian, but we want you to know that." Since that meeting, Bill had read about Correct Craft's bout with bankruptcy in the company history, *Saved from Bankruptcy.* He was impressed by the testimonies of the miracle boat production and the Meloons' stand during bankruptcy. "That was good for me in considering the faith, even though I didn't talk directly with them," he says.

The day after his salvation experience, Snook returned to Correct Craft to continue a ten-week period of working through the manufacturing plant. He was doing many of the different factory jobs in order to better know the product. At the end of the ten weeks, he finally had a chance to meet W. O. and Ralph.

Their warmth and concern did not surprise him. And he thinks the company's policy to tend to the spiritual needs of employees like himself is balanced and fair—good news indeed.

Notes

1. Jim Harmon, "The Meloons: Three Parts Know-How, Three Parts Faith," *Powerboat,* August 1982, 47.
2. The other five are: love and the competitive drive, people needs and profit obligations, humility and the ego of success, family and work, and charity and wealth. See Laura L. Nash, *Believers in Business* (Nashville: Nelson, 1994).
3. Ibid., 249–61.
4. "Letters," *Nautique News,* fall/winter 1994, 2.
5. Nash, *Believers in Business,* 256.

Chapter 14

On the Waters of the World

*T*he business card of the 1990s has gone high tech. No longer listing just a name and title, the card can be four-color, embossed in gold leaf, have clever computer-designed logos, depict the company or individual's talents, and even include a three-dimensional hologram.

If business cards are printed to create a good first impression, no one does it better than Ralph Meloon and his brother W. O. Their slick, one-fold card features a color photo of a Ski Nautique in action on the cover, with the man's name and title on the back. When a recipient opens the card, he or she reads the following:

> It has been a pleasure meeting you. May I share with you a little about our company and myself?
>
> My father began building boats more than 60 years ago. We are one of the oldest family-owned boat manufacturing companies in the United States. We believe we manufacture one of the finest lines of recreational boats with inboard engines. They are owned and enjoyed by several kings and rulers of various nations. Correct Craft boats are used as Official Water Ski Tow Boats in more than 80 percent of the Water Ski Tournaments around the world.

Every one of our boats starts in a master mold. The craftsmen know how to put it all together, and the raw material soon turns out to be another quality boat.

As a young man, I discovered from the Bible that there is a Master Builder, God Himself. He can take a man's life, no matter how rough it seems to be, and create a new life which will be beautiful and useful. Life has been worth living since I asked Jesus Christ to become the Master Builder of my life and to recreate in me a new life which would be pleasing to Him.

He will do the same for you if you ask Him. Please write me if I can be of help to you.

Sincerely,
Ralph Meloon, Sr.

Both men still travel, Ralph much more than W. O., and they continue to distribute the cards. The testimonial inside shows their dual passion: to spur sales of Correct Craft boats and to introduce all they meet to the God of the Bible, who offers everyone a personal relationship through Jesus Christ. They give credit for the card to the former editor of *Nautique News* (then the *Orlando Tribune*), Don Moreland. The editor first suggested that Walt put his Christian testimony inside so that he would be sure everyone who received a card heard the Meloons' story and their praise to God. Moreland offered suggestions, and W. O. developed it. Ralph, impressed with the card, prepared a similar one for his business and personal contacts.

The card was first printed in 1978, and the elder Meloons have distributed thousands since, both in the U. S. and abroad. Ralph has also prepared a more in-depth gospel tract that includes the story of Correct Craft's role in putting the first commercial water skis into production. He gives the tract to waiters, waitresses, tour guides, and others (along with a healthy tip). Entitled "Boat Builder Meets the Life Builder," the tract is published in Russian, French, German, Spanish, Korean, and English.

Perhaps the company's slogan, "On the Waters of the

World since 1925," has two meanings. The company has been selling boats worldwide, and its executives have been ambassadors for Christ in international settings, for several decades.

Its international sales also give the company a buffer against U. S. economic downturns. "Boats are going into Russia, China, and Japan," says Mike Elrod, the production vice president. "I'm a believer that pennies equal nickels, and nickels equal dimes, and so on. So you send two boats a year into Russia. That helps. The king of Jordan buys two every other year. You send three over here. We're selling six there. All that adds up. During a downturn, we're selling all over the world."

INTERNATIONAL NEGOTIATIONS

The company typically has been wise in its international negotiations. Ralph praises W. N. for directing the research and development, "which gives us the finest product on the market," and for being "very on-target in his decisions for our international business."

For instance, the two men strengthened Correct Craft's position in Japan in 1995 after five years of limited success. The breakthrough came when Correct Craft realized that two of its Japanese dealers were unethical. They had alienated the country's largest dealer of ski boats by using a "See him, buy from us" strategy. The largest dealer, Mr. Suzuki, sold boats from Correct Craft and a major rival. The two smaller dealers would send prospective customers to Suzuki's showroom to see more Correct Craft models and colors than they offered. When the customers returned, the smaller dealers would beat Suzuki's price.

Suzuki, who had the better selection and spent much time showing the boat's features, lost sales time after time. As a result, he continued to stock boats of the rival boat maker and felt frustrated that Correct Craft had dealers who would undercut him and use his sales staff to promote the boat before stealing the sale.

Ralph filed a report after he returned from an international boat show in Japan. Later he told W. N., "Walt, you'll never get Mr. Suzuki to give up his rival boats, because he sells more of them than he does Ski Nautiques. He likes our boats better, but he will never do it."

When W. N. understood why Suzuki had lower sales of Correct Craft boats, he discussed the implications with Ralph. He decided to send two company officials to negotiate with Suzuki at the Chicago Boat Show. Eventually, Correct Craft decided to make Suzuki the sole distributor in Japan. In return, Suzuki agreed to stock only Correct Craft boats.

The decision benefited Suzuki, who obtained exclusive domestic rights to market Correct Craft boats, and the company, which saw Japanese sales climb steadily. In fact, Suzuki's large dealership soon was selling more Correct Craft boats in one year than the other two dealers combined had sold. It was another example of a decision motivated by ethics: Correct Craft insisted on the same treatment by its dealers that the company displayed to its customers and employees.

In all their world travels, however, the Meloons have been alert to spiritual opportunities as much as sales opportunities. W. O. was named the 1979 "Man of the Year" by the National Association of Evangelicals for his leadership of the national men's program of the Christian and Missionary Alliance (CMA).

As president of that program in 1976, he helped to organize major relief efforts in Guatemala that year, after the devastating February 4 earthquake ruined buildings, bridges, and roads. More than 20,000 Guatemalans were either seriously injured or killed in the temblor, which measured 7.5 on the Richter scale. Construction teams of thirty to forty men, armed with their own hammers, saws, and levels, helped rebuild several churches. Men who couldn't go donated $300,000 for emergency help. The planning and initiative by W. O. Meloon and others also firmed up the groundwork for later projects in other countries.

W. O. also undertook a five-week venture in the Far East, including the Philippines, Hong Kong, and Taiwan, on behalf of the Alliance Men (of the CMA). Earlier, he had joined the Billy Graham Evangelistic Association for twelve weeks in the Far East, including Japan, Thailand, and Singapore. During the Graham Crusade in the Philippines, he spoke at auto assembly plants and in street meetings. He also distributed many of his business cards to Filipino passersby.

There in the Philippines, he noticed a strange phenomenon. After reading the final line of his testimony, "Please write me if I can be a help to you," a number of people thought that meant Meloon would give them money. Perhaps that was because of the image of the rich American. But the requests have not been limited to Filipinos, W. O. reports. Over the years, he has received dozens of letters with a similar message: "Thank you for your promise of help. I need [this amount of money]."

The feeling that money will solve everyone's problems recurs in most countries W. O. has visited, even primitive ones. He believes the lure of money is a ploy Satan uses across cultures, not just in America. "Satan has done a great job of promoting the love of money around the world," he says. "One of the biggest desires is to have more money. 'How do I get more money?' is the question they ask. As Jesus said, 'You can't worship mammon and Me too.'"

AN EYEWITNESS TO FAITH AND PERSECUTION

The Meloons' overseas tours in search of sales and souls have also been encouraging, especially as they've met other Christians. Many believers in China and in Muslim countries have strong faith because of the persecution they face. A missionary in Kuwait once told Ralph that a Kuwaiti Muslim had become a Christian. At first, the new Christian remained silent in order to avoid persecution. But he finally decided he would attend the Christian church. When his neighbors learned he had been to the church, "they nailed him," Ralph says. "But he stood up for what he believed."

As a result, Kuwaiti officials threatened him. "They said,

'Well, you ought to be beheaded.' He still stood up for his faith. I haven't heard the outcome," Ralph reports.

Ralph also remembers Huda Masha, whom he met while in Jordan. A close friend of King Hussein, "she gets on the phone with me because she wants the Christians praying for her while she is here. She is strong for the Lord.

"So you do meet the strong Christians who will stand up and be counted for the Lord. God still lets them live in many cases."

But Ralph has been in Saudi Arabia on Fridays, too, when the Islamic courts mete out justice. Those convicted have hands cut off for stealing or are beheaded for murder or religious heresy—being a Christian.

Such persecution has been a powerful form of evangelism, Ralph believes: "Persecution is what wins people to Christ. Go into Eastern Europe and there are many underground Christians. Go into Western Europe and there are hardly any, because their faith is free."

In Ralph's travels for Correct Craft, he has had many evangelistic opportunities, including at international tournaments. At the 1993 World Championships in Singapore, for example, Correct Craft and Ralph organized "The Night of Champions." In a sense, it was an encore presentation, for the company had held a similar public gathering during the 1989 World Championship in Toulouse, France.

Though Correct Craft enjoys being selected as the official towboat of international competitions, Ralph says, "Each time our boats have been chosen, it has been very expensive for us to fulfill that responsibility. So we have also tried to go to the site ahead of time to develop a time for the Christian water-skiers to share their faith with the people in the host country."

"THE NIGHT OF CHAMPIONS"

Working with Baptist missionaries in Singapore as well as local pastors, Correct Craft officials spent nine months organizing "The Night of Champions." They scheduled the event for

Friday night, just before the final day of the week-long competition. That would draw youth, they reasoned, as would the local Christian musicians on the program. But the real draw would be three outstanding skiers: Kristi Overton, consistently one of the top three women skiers in America; Mike Suyderhoud, former overall world champion and coach of the American team; and Harold Cole, once the top freestyle skier in the world.

The skiers' accomplishments almost became the undoing of the program. Suyderhoud had been named to the International World Hall of Fame by the International Water Ski Federation (IWSF), and after saying yes to "The Night of Champions," he was notified the induction ceremony would be the same Friday night. He couldn't snub the IWSF and certainly wanted to say thank you for the honor. Ralph scheduled a meeting with an IWSF official that Friday morning and explained the situation. The official agreed to delay the presentation thirty minutes. Ralph then moved Suyderhoud to the front of the program, and after he spoke, the hall of famer was whisked to the hotel for the induction ceremony.

Cole gave the closing testimony at "The Night of Champions," inviting people to make a decision for Christ. At least ten people responded. "They say this is remarkable, because you just don't get the [Singapore] people to make decisions that quickly," Ralph notes.

"We thank God that He does give us the opportunity to build the finest water-ski boat in the world, and we pray that we will be faithful in our responsibility to Him to share our faith and introduce as many people as possible to our wonderful Savior, Jesus," Ralph adds.

In September 1990, Ralph attended the Friendship Cup, the waterskiing championship of the entire socialist world. It would be the final Friendship Cup, as citizens were rebelling against communist governments in the East; Mikhail Gorbachev was about to watch the USSR split into many independent republics. Ralph talked about his faith wherever government officials took him in Ukraine and Moscow. He later learned his greatest impact was not on a ski tournament official but on a young woman guard at the Museum of Arts in Kiev.

On his way through the museum, he had given her a business card. Seven months later, he received a letter from Marina that began with two Scripture verses, Matthew 4:19-20: "And he saith unto them, Follow me, and I will make you fishers of men. And they straightway left their nets, and followed him" (KJV). Ralph read her letter with keen interest:

> You remember how you were His fisherman in Kiev, USSR, last summer and how your divine net caught a Ukrainian girl in the Museum of Arts. You gave me your card with information about yourself and your life with Jesus Christ. It was the biggest impression of all, and remembering your happy eyes and beautiful words about our Savior, I began looking for the Bible. And after a lot of toil I was lucky to buy one. I wanted to learn to understand the truth and to become happy, and my heart was filled with joy.
>
> I studied the book and shared it with my friends. I shared my knowledge with those who thought that they may become happy by having more and more material things. I kept telling them that material things couldn't give us eternal life and happiness with our Father and His Son, that everyone who accepted the knowledge would be forever with them. It was quite an effort to do that because I am not an experienced teacher, but anyway I helped some and I feel happy about that.

"This letter thrilled me very much," Ralph says. Later Marina tried without success to attend a U. S. Bible college, though a close friend was able to study at Toccoa Falls Bible College (Toccoa, Georgia).

Van Thurston, the executive director of Turnaround Ministries, remembers watching Ralph talk about Jesus while on a flight in Argentina. The Meloons were holding their first Turnaround Weekends outside the U. S. in 1996, and during the flight from Buenos Aires to Cordova, Ralph gave tracts to most of the passengers. (The "Boat Builder" tract was in Spanish, of course.)

"The flight attendants get them and read them and thank him," Van says. "Four days later, when we fly back to Buenos Aires, the same flight attendants are on board. When the plane levels off, here come the flight attendants. They get Ralph and put him in the cockpit. He stayed in the cockpit until we were at the gate in Buenos Aires, talking to the pilots about the Lord.

"It turned out the pilots had seen the tracts, courtesy of one of the attendants, and wanted to talk to him. In the cockpit, they engaged him about his work at Correct Craft, and he talked about that and his favorite subject, the creator God and His love for them."

No decisions were made that day, but in the plane, some 25,000 feet above sea level, Ralph had presented the gospel with boldness and love.

Once, after Ralph flew to a conference, Van asked him, "Why don't you fly up front in first class, where you can rest and feel better?"

"Oh, Van! There's only twelve people up front," Ralph said. "There's 100 in the back. I can walk up and down those aisles and give out tracts all day."

"And he does!" Van says with admiration.

Interestingly, W. N. Meloon does not carry a testimony on his business card, choosing to use a more standard card. "That may change as I get older and maybe my role changes and I do more traveling overseas," he says. But his concern for the spiritual needs of those he meets is no less. He simply prefers the indirect approach.

When a businessman or friend describes something good that has happened, more than once W. N. has said, "Well, aren't you lucky. I know God's been very good to me."

"That's a great opener in a conversation," W. N. explains. At times, people have complimented him for the company's success and how good he must feel about coming so far from the bankruptcy. W. N.'s response? "That's the perfect opportuni-

ty to say, 'By the grace of God, there have been benefits that have
been around for the family and me.' There are thousands of
ways to open a conversation about the Lord. Dad and Ralph's
way is very effective, however, and I wouldn't argue that for a
moment."

PRAYERS OF FAITH

Now almost eighty, Ralph continues to travel and talk
about his faith. Most waterskiing officials know of his faith, and
at tournaments and other events, either he or W. O. is called on
to give an invocation or express thanks to God before a meal.
Occasionally, Ralph has been called upon to intercede with
God. Ralph doesn't think he has a special pipeline to God, yet
his faith moves people toward God, and at times, his faith is
even stretched by God.

There was, for example, the major tournament in
Guadalajara, Mexico, in 1994. Soon after he and other Correct
Craft officials arrived, it began to rain. The rain would let up,
only to return again. The tournament quickly fell behind schedule. Skiing in the rain posed safety hazards because of lightning
in the area. And during heavier rains, competitiors could not
easily see the buoys or the approach to the jump ramp.

Finally, several tournament officials approached Ralph
and said, "Mr. Meloon, we would like to have you pray and ask
God to take the rain away so we can finish the tournament."

"I will be praying; I always pray at night," Ralph
answered. "But I have enough problems trying to run a boat
business, so I'm not going to try to dabble in God's business."

The next morning, he returned to the competition site,
and the rains had resumed. Soon some officials approached
him. "Mr. Meloon, didn't you pray?" they asked.

"Yes, I prayed, and I asked the Lord to let His will be
done," he answered. "I did ask Him to allow us to have a good
tournament, and one with no accidents or injuries to the skiers.
I said, 'Lord, You know all about everything, and we're not

going to try to run Your business. We're just going to do the best we can with what You give us.'"

The rains continued another ten minutes. Then "the weather cleared up and we had no more bad weather the rest of the time," Ralph reports. By beginning several events early, officials got in a complete tournament. And Ralph Meloon once again saw His faithful God at work on the waters of the world.

Chapter 15
Ski the Yangtze

*T*he Yangtze River (pronounced *yank see*) flows 3,500
miles from the Kunlun Mountains in the western
province of Tsinghai eastward into the East China Sea.
It is alternately friend and foe to the residents of the People's
Republic of China, commonly known as mainland China. The
river irrigates crops, but it can also flood the surrounding land
during summer storms. And in all of China, some of the best
waterskiing occurs in its delta area at the port city of Shanghai.

Not that there's a lot of skiing in mainland China. Most
people don't know how, and there are few ski boats available.
But that may change soon, thanks to the efforts of Correct Craft
and ski officials to bring waterskiing to the country.

W. O. Meloon visited mainland China twice in the 1980s,
and Ralph went two other times. Ralph also visited the Republic
of China, better known as Taiwan, once and attended a historic
meeting between mainland China's and Taiwan's ski officials in
1989. Along the way, Correct Craft officials and the Meloons
dispensed training, boats, and advice that helped the countries
move forward in their ski programs. Their adventures in the
two countries are studies in diplomacy, advances in sport, and
the Meloons' passion for their sport and their God.

W. O's first visit was a fact-finding trip on the state of

waterskiing and the church in mainland China. Businessman John Bechtel, born in China of missionary parents and fluent in Chinese, accompanied him, and they distributed Bibles and met with officials of China's water ski federation. The two men were honored at banquets and receptions, and W. O. received help as he looked for closed churches that had existed before the Chinese revolution of 1949. He found only the remains of one Southern Baptist church, but he met many Christians who had survived and thrived in "underground" house churches.

Upon leaving, W. O. invited officials to send a water-ski delegation to America as guests of Correct Craft. They agreed, and within a year skier Xiang Qinhai, accompanied by his coach and an interpreter, was in Florida, seeing Correct Craft boats being made and spending two weeks at a Windermere, Florida ski school. There he improved his slalom and trick skiing skills and learned how to jump.

In July 1985, two Chinese officials returned as guests of Correct Craft to watch the Masters ski tournament at Callaway Gardens in Georgia. China's first ski tournament was imminent, and they watched closely and asked questions of company officials, as Correct Craft was a cosponsor of the tournament.

Ralph Meloon went to China in 1986 with engineer Bill Snook and a new Ski Nautique. They would demonstrate the boat, train drivers, and leave at least this boat with the Chinese. Before they began, Bill broke the ice among strangers when he asked for a snack. The interpreter misheard Bill, and he may have been unfamiliar with the American expression for a light meal. So he translated the word "snake." His hosts looked at him strangely and were perhaps ready to find some snake meat when Bill and the translator checked their signals. The translator finally communicated clearly, and everyone laughed. The party seemed to warm up to the young American at the elder Meloon's side.

Bill demonstrated how to grease the wheel bearings on the boat trailer. Then Ralph and he invited the Chinese delegation to a demonstration on the lake. At first, though, the officials didn't want a demonstration, thinking that the drive and boat launching would be too difficult.

"If you want to learn how to use these, we need to see you launch it and do everything so we can help you," Bill explained. The Chinese finally agreed, and so began a convoy of minivans and jeeps on a winding, dirt road. They passed little tractors and bicycles and saw occasional army trucks. At one point a jeep broke down, and Bill found his Craftsman tools and helped to repair the vehicle. The inexperienced drivers soon had the vans in fifth gear again at fifteen miles per hour. "Once the driver got a head of steam, he was going to pass anything that got in the way," Bill recalls. "We were passing on hills and curves. It was positively frightening."

Finally they descended to a most beautiful setting—a volcanic crater lake, with a sandy shore and deep, blue water. But then Bill watched as nearly a dozen men walked to the lake.

"What are they going to do?" he asked his interpreter.

"They're going to put the boat in the water."

"How are they going to do that?"

"Well, they're going to lift the boat from the trailer and carry it."

"No, wait," Bill said. "There's a better way. Let me show you."

The interpreter yelled, and the men stopped arranging ropes on the boat. Bill motioned the jeep driver to back the boat trailer to the water's edge. Bill then started the engine, put it in reverse, and let the boat slide into the water. He immediately heard oohs and aahs from the men on the beach, who now knew there was an easier way to transport the boat to the water.

Ralph took the controls and waited for several officials to get into the boat, but he watched in amazement as the entire Chinese delegation began to clamber aboard—all twenty-five people.

"Hey, we can't do that!" Ralph exclaimed, and the parade of people halted. Somehow, though, about twelve fit into the boat for the first ride. The rest watched from shore as Ralph added throttle.

AN EYE-OPENER

"When I hit the throttle, I'm telling you, they had never had a sensation like that in all their lives," Ralph says. "Their eyes almost popped. When the boat accelerated and lifted from the water, it felt like 100 miles per hour."

In fact, the Correct Craft veteran had quickly accelerated the boat to forty miles per hour. The boat moved smoothly across the lake.

"When I got to the far end of the lake, to me there was nothing to it, but these guys felt like they had been on a Ferris wheel for the first time," Ralph says. "Then I turned the steering wheel to head back, and when the boat banked in the turn— oh, they really went crazy! They were impressed and scared."

Bill disagrees slightly with his boss. "He opened it up," Bill insists. "Ralph's got a reputation for being a hotshot driver. He didn't baby them in the turn. He let the boat do what it can do."

Many of the Chinese had not been on a powerboat before, including a woman who spoke excellent English and later said she was scared by the acceleration and handling.

The visit was a success, including the potential of leaving behind inboard powerboats. (The government later ordered eighteen boats for its ski team.) Bill instructed drivers on maintenance procedures. Then the two Americans continued to Kuei-lin, Shanghai, and other towns. During the trip, they distributed water skis and films on skiing. In Shanghai, Ralph led a tour guide to Christ.

After the visit, Correct Craft made arrangements for follow-up training for skiers, and especially for drivers. Eighteen months later, Les and Cindy Todd went to train Chinese skiers for international competition. The Todds are talented water-skiers, and Les was one of America's finest drivers at the time. "We sent two Christian water-skiers to teach them to water-ski and get the gospel in also," Ralph explains.

The Chinese contact later called the Todds "the ideal coaches whom the Chinese skiers are eager to have." He may have said that knowing that Les was a skilled boat driver, because the Todds soon learned that the Chinese' skiing ability exceeded their driving ability. "It ended up the Chinese needed someone to drive the boat more than they needed someone to teach them to ski," Ralph notes. The few drivers available didn't know how to handle the throttle, and the boats often lurched forward. Typically, a driver would "throw the throttle down and just yank the arms out of the kids. They didn't have a chance to get up," Ralph says.

Cindy, a world champion water-skier for many years, helped train nine skiers from six provinces, including six women. And Les taught the few drivers on the Chinese team.

THE TAIWANESE GYMNASTS

Despite their success in mainland China, however, Ralph could not forget his first visit to China's rival, Taiwan, one year earlier. In 1985, he met officials of the country's water ski federation on the island nation. His purpose was to describe the popularity of waterskiing worldwide and to promote greater interest. At the time of his visit, skiers in Taiwan's ski federation were learning new stunts for show skiing. But the highlight was his guest lecture at a local all-girls gymnastics class, arranged by the federation secretary, who taught the class.

Joey Chow introduced the guest, and the seventy girls, age thirteen and dressed in their practice leotards, paid close attention. "They respect age," Ralph recalls. "When someone is old enough to have gray hair, they really respect you."

Ralph began by discussing show skiing: skiers riding atop other skiers, making fancy turns. "It's not easy," he told the girls. "The man is on a slalom ski, has the top-heavy weight of someone on his shoulders, and then he still skis."

He described show skiing, and Joey's wife, Jackie, continued to translate his words. "Now you will be doing it here," Ralph said. "Now you will be doing exhibitions." He went on to express his faith in God and the importance of knowing God through Jesus Christ. He concluded by offering a book to anyone who would write him. Three of the girls did, and they were contacted by Teyet Moy, the son of a Correct Craft employee and now a missionary in Taiwan. Teyet delivered the book, entitled *On the Waters of the World,* with accompanying letters in Chinese that talked about Christ. The three girls, all Buddhists, expressed further interest, and Ralph began to write.

All three are now Christians. Paula Lin wrote Ralph in 1989, thanking him for a book about David Livingstone:

> I am deeply impressed and encouraged by his missionary experience and devotion to God's work in Africa. I had the same feeling when reading the biography of Hudson Taylor. The truth has been made transparent to me that devotion and submission are the only way to be used by the Lord. . . .
>
> I have to tell you, Mr. Meloon, that to be thoroughly submissive is a difficult thing to be learned. When I become restless and disturbed, I have to turn to the Lord anew and ask for fresh grace. I pray, as one of my favorite hymns says, for being treated like a baby, who knows nothing except what lies between a mother's warm arms in total dependence and rest.

When Ralph later visited Taipei in 1993, he invited Paula and the two other girls, Jennifer Huang and Nancy Wang, to meet with him. Only Jennifer could join him. Paula now lived far from Taipei, and Nancy was studying at the University of Chicago. Nancy sent Ralph a Christmas card in 1993 with a letter that revealed her heart for her homeland:

> I'll stay in Taiwan for a long time until the Lord sends me elsewhere. Please pray for the opening of mainland China, which is seemingly polite and tolerant but rejecting the Bible and threatening a lot of Jesus-loving missionaries.
>
> Thank you for your good wishes. This is the Word I enjoyed today: "Bless those who persecute you. Bless and do not curse." Romans 12:14
>
> Love in Christ

In May 1989, Ralph returned to mainland China to break bread with ski federation officials from both the People's Republic of China and the Republic of China, two political antagonists who at least seemed to have common ground on China's lakes. President Yi Hou-Gao of the Chinese Water Ski Federation requested Ralph's presence at the meal and then at their first international ski tournament. Ralph agreed and was accompanied by a friend, J. D. Brown, after Ralph's wife decided not to go.

But like all trips he takes overseas, Ralph's journey had another purpose as well. He wanted to present the gospel of Jesus Christ.

"We are always to speak about the Lord," Ralph says. "And He gave us the Ski Nautique to get us in the door. So we'd better do what He tells us to do. Of course, they [the Chinese] would not invite me over to get the gospel out; they invited me to attend the tournament." So he planned to do both.

TWO "ENEMIES" FACE-TO-FACE

At a memorable dinner, officials from the two sports federations, Ralph Meloon, and J. D. Brown sat at a large, round table. Ralph was seated to the right of Yi, the president of mainland China's sports federation. To Yi's left was the president of the water ski federation of Taiwan, Shih Chen Liu. To Meloon's right was his translator. Other officials were seated around the table, with J. D. positioned at the farthest point, directly across from President Yi.

"It was good to sit at the table with two countries—archenemies—talking about waterskiing, education, and anything but war. Only a few years previously, the People's Republic had vowed to take over Taiwan and make it part of them," Ralph says.

Ralph believes the goodwill at that table reflected the goodwill of the citizens of both countries. "I think every country has a lot of wonderful people," he says. "The ones who are the troublemakers are those at the top. They want glory and money.

They don't believe in religion, but they want to be God—they want to dictate everything. But they aren't capable of that because they *aren't* God."

Among the Chinese leaders at the table, however, there was only respect for the Meloons—for Walt O. and his brother Ralph. The Chinese hosts knew the Meloons had helped the Taiwanese and realized the water ski federation of Taiwan was not interested in politics. And they remembered the fun of being with the Americans three years earlier, especially with Bill Snook, Correct Craft's chief engineer, who at age thirty-two was near the age of the Chinese skiers.

Ironically, Ralph was unable to attend China's first international waterskiing tournament. The night before the event, he was rushed from his hotel room to a hospital, suffering from internal bleeding. A specialist, Dr. Guo-Zong Pan, soon found the problem with the help of a scope. Ralph's entire stomach appeared ulcerated, and the doctor and other medical consultants tracked it to his anti-inflammatory medicine. Ralph had been taking Motrin for fifteen years to get relief from chronic arthritis and bursitis. Anti-inflammatory medications have been known to irritate stomach linings.

They discontinued the medicine, but what about the blood loss? China had problems with tainted blood from hepatitis B, so they hesitated to give Ralph many transfusions. "We are going to give as little blood as possible," Dr. Pan explained. "The more we give, the more the chance you will get something bad. We have hardly any AIDS here, but we do have hepatitis B. That's just as bad—either one can kill you."

Using limited blood transfusion and monitoring his stomach's healing, they built up Ralph's blood supply. In one week, his blood count was high enough for his release from the hospital. The tournament was over, though a trip to Hong Kong remained on his itinerary. But Ralph was too weak and returned home. He made a full recovery, and four months later he was able to fly to Russia on business.

Before he left the hospital, he had presented the gospel

through his tracts and personal testimony to everyone he met. The final day, as Dr. Pan came to say good-bye, Ralph talked about his blood crisis.

"Remember the first day that I was here and you said you were going to give me some Chinese blood?" he asked. "You told me China had problems with blood, just like we have in the United States. You said that the blood is not always perfect, so you suggested I take only as little as possible.

"How true your words were, because the blood of man is not perfect, and at best the blood is only going to supply me life for another fifteen to twenty years. But I can tell you about a blood that *is* perfect. The blood of the Lord Jesus Christ that was shed on the cross for our sins is the perfect blood that will give you life—not for ten or twenty years, but for eternity."

His words made an impression on the doctor. In 1991, Dr. Pan visited the United States, and although Ralph could not meet with him, they talked on the phone.

"Doctor, I want to thank you again for saving my life while I was in China," the boatbuilder said.

"We didn't save your life. God saved it," Dr. Pan answered.

Recalling that conversation, Ralph concludes, "That was the first clue I had that Dr. Pan had changed his mind after I had shared with him at the hospital. Now I feel certain he knows the Lord as his Savior."

Since Correct Craft's visits in the 1980s, the People's Republic of China has made a steady improvement in waterskiing. At one point, the national tournament team placed eleventh in the world. Since then, the team performance has declined, as the government decided to promote and fund Olympic sports, which they believed had greater visibility. That could change if the International Olympic Committee (IOC) decides to make waterskiing an Olympic event. IOC officials viewed the water-ski competition during the 1995 Pan American Games in Santa Fe, Argentina, and came away impressed.

The committee still hesitates, though, to sanction water-skiing either as an exhibition sport or an official sport of the

Olympic Games because of the role of the driver. It believes the driver has too much influence on the skier's performance. To address that issue in the 1994 Pan American Games, the water-ski competition adapted a speed control to limit the driver's role.

Bill Snook calls the issue "a huge hurdle" to getting water-ski competition into the Olympics. He points to the luge and bobsled, two events in the Winter Games, as having drivers as well, yet their vehicles are under the direct control of the competitors. The solution, according to Snook, is to make the boat driver and water-skier part of one team so that "the driver and the skier both earn the medal. Let the driver drive within the rules, and let him help the skier, as long as he stays within the rules. That might be a way to overcome the issue. Until they do that, I don't see waterskiing becoming an Olympic sport."

Not until that happens is the Chinese government likely to support a ski team. "We must continue the program basically through private funding," a woman official told Snook at the '95 World Water Ski Championship in Toulouse, France. "That is difficult to do." Snook says that even without government support, however, the Chinese team shows some promise in trick skiing.

A SHANGHAI SKI COURSE

So what's the likelihood that the Chinese will ski the Yangtze soon? Since the sale of the nineteen boats, Correct Craft has sold several more to mainland China. But few boats are entering China now, as the government has slapped on heavy import duties.

Still, wealthy farmers may soon have a greater interest in consumer goods, such as cars and boats. The People's Republic has to feed 1.2 billion people; less than 12 percent of its land is tillable; and the government has achieved unusual success with incentives to farmers, turning more than a few into rich men. The government, desperate to motivate the farmers to produce more with little acreage, agreed to let the farmers keep a portion for themselves once they met a quota. And U. S. agricultural experts invited to China have shown the farmers techniques for increasing their harvest. As a result, the farmers learned how to boost their wheat yield. Soon they had bumper crops—record harvests—that the government had not anticipated.

"[Communist leader] Deng had not set the crop standards high enough. So these farmers began making money, and they ended up being millionaires," Ralph says. Farmers who were making a dollar a day under the old system have flourished under this modified form of free enterprise that lets them sell to the general public a portion of their crops.

Of course, most of the farmers don't think first of buying boats. Equipment for improving crop yields and automobiles are at the top of their wish lists. But as waterskiing grows in popularity, Ralph anticipates the farmers will have an interest in ski boats. Already the Chinese have added Jet Skis to the paddleboats on their lakes. Towboats seem the next likely progression. Correct Craft hopes to have a Chinese importer establish a network of dealers in the late 1990s.

Meanwhile, much of the waterskiing occurs in the Yangtze delta area at Shanghai. Several calm, open waters in the delta would be suitable for slalom courses. The East China Sea is nearby, but the waves die at the reeds guarding the entrance to the river. Ralph expects a ski course there one day, just as there are dozens of slalom courses outside Buenos Aires, where the Rio de la Plata ends in the Atlantic Ocean.

So one day, enthusiasts may ski the Yangtze. And when they do, there's a good chance the boat of choice will be a Ski Nautique. Once more, the Meloons and Correct Craft will be parting the waters of the world.

Epilogue
Business Principles
That Work

For almost seventy-five years, Walter C. Meloon, his sons, and his grandson have presided over America's oldest family-owned boatbuilding business. From early on, they have operated the company according to biblical principles, desiring to honor God. Looking at their mission statement, policies, and the example of these executives, several business principles stand out. Here are ten that have been demonstrated by the Meloons for three generations:

1. *Perform all work to honor God first and make a profit second. When the two purposes clash, always choose God over profit.* W. N. never makes changes with the profit motive foremost in mind. "I don't want to change just for the sake of money," he says. Instead, changes are made to improve an already top-quality product and to honor God.

"When people suggest to me that there are cheaper ways to build our boats, I must consider the compromises that would have to be made. As Christians, we should never compromise our faith; therefore to compromise the quality of this product would be a disservice to all who benefit from it." W. N. says Correct Craft boats "have earned a reputation for quality that is unmatched in the marine industry."

Honoring God also means demonstrating personal

integrity in all business transactions. The company chose to face financial crisis—and eventual bankruptcy—rather than pay a boat inspector a bribe. The Meloons believe a good reputation is good business and has a lasting Christian testimony. Today the company is a leader in the inboard boating industry. *Shortcuts* and *compromise* are not part of its vocabulary. In fact, within the boating industry, "One hears such terms as 'honesty,' 'character' and 'integrity' in the descriptions of the Meloons," according to *Powerboat* magazine.

2. *Serve nonalcoholic beverages at company functions.* Though Scripture does not forbid an occasional drink, the Meloons believe the policy of neither serving nor drinking alcoholic beverages sends a clear signal of their devotion to God and helps others—employees, suppliers, and dealers—to have one less temptation to strong drink. They respectfully decline drinks in social settings.

3. *Honor the Lord by observing a day of rest.* Businesses not offering essential services should be closed at least one day a week, the Meloons are convinced. No work should be scheduled on Sundays, when private and public worship of God can take place. This Sunday observance reflects a desire to honor God. It also allows all workers to be refreshed and thus more productive for the next workweek.

4. *Develop corporate policies that reflect Christian values.* The *Reader's Digest* profile of Correct Craft (see chapter 7) lauded the company as one that observes the Golden Rule: Treat others as you want to be treated. Such treatment has resulted in management offering fair benefits to employees and demonstrating integrity and honesty to employees, suppliers, and dealers alike. Managers model compassion in their relationships. In its advertising, Correct Craft rejects photos that sell its boats by sex appeal; in its sponsorships, the company shuns major alliances with alcohol companies, even though beer companies sponsor many skiing tournaments.

5. *Honor the legacy of the company.* As the second and third presidents of Correct Craft, Ralph and Walt O. honored their

father and founder of the company and desired to honor God by producing a quality product. W. N. honors the previous leaders as he extends their boatbuilding standards. "We have maintained the standards of excellence set by our founder, W. C. Meloon," President Walter N. Meloon wrote in the 1997 catalog. "His tenet for doing business was very basic, 'offer your customer the best product, the finest materials and build it to the glory of God.'"

6. *Believe in and promote the business.* Whether the business provides goods or services, corporate leaders should participate in industry developments and promote growth of the industry. Doing so not only makes good business sense in terms of more sales, but it also should be a natural outcome of enthusiasm for your business.

As a major ski boat manufacturer, Correct Craft has been a leading supporter of water-skiers since 1961, when it offered top skiers the use of its boats for promotional consideration. Ralph continues to travel worldwide to promote ski tournaments and skiing. W. N. has served as president of the American Water Ski Educational Foundation (AWSEF). The Meloon family has been lauded in trade magazines for its devotion to the sport. And in 1994, the AWSEF presented W. O., Ralph, and W. N. Meloon the Award of Distinction for their work in promoting professional and recreational skiing.

7. *Work hard, giving your best effort.* A successful business requires much energy. Some experts suggest that a new business requires the owner to work sixty to seventy hours a week, and that a business typically has to operate two years before the owner can expect a profit. But managers should continue to give maximum effort even after the business is established. This sets an example and reflects the biblical injunction that we work "with all your heart, as working for the Lord" (Colossians 3:23).

W. C. Meloon began his days at 5 A.M., and son W. O. put in long hours years before he became president. Those hours varied from an almost regular nine hours to "until the sun went down" during the busy times. And W. O.'s hours did not diminish much just before his retirement. "You do what you have to do, whether it takes a day or more," he says.

But W. O. emphasizes that work hours should not preclude time with God. In fact, time spent with God is vital in making good decisions. "I learned, especially after the bankruptcy proceedings began, that prayer time is more important than people time," he says. In the mornings, before he left for work, "I got through my devotions with my wife and brought before the Lord all the problems. Sometimes I'd look at the clock and say, 'Oh my goodness, I had an appointment half an hour ago!' and rush to work."

8. *Always repay your creditors.* Paying debts is a biblical principle. The Meloons have honored that principle through the generations, beginning with Walt C. repaying a banker's widow years after a garage fire destroyed his inventories and left him unable to repay the loan promptly. He worked two shifts to be able to do that.

When the bankruptcy judge ordered Correct Craft to pay its remaining creditors 20 percent of the balance owed, the Meloons did that, but then they spent the next twenty-five years paying off the other 80 percent as well. "My dad said, 'If you have a man's money and you haven't paid it back, you still owe it,'" says W. O. Meloon. Ralph and W. O. had come to the same conclusion that repaying all creditors 100 percent was the right thing to do. W. O. says it's an issue of ethics: "It's a question of right or wrong—one thing is wrong; the other thing is right."

9. *Return your bounty to the Lord.* Every businessperson should contribute to charities and missions from the company's profits. Correct Craft donates 10 percent of its profits to such organizations, and the president and former presidents give from their personal incomes as well. In addition, the company has given boats to missions and has a special program for selling boats at a discount to camps and college water-ski teams.

Such giving makes good business sense, as a businessperson recognizes that all he or she has comes through God's blessings. "In reality, we don't own anything. It all belongs to

God," Ralph emphasizes. "We're just returning to Him what He has given us. God doesn't need the money. He needs us as servants. But money is one way He helps those who preach the gospel. We ought to return it."

Ralph was impressed by Christian industrialist R. G. LeTourneau, who in later years reportedly gave away more than 90 percent of his annual income to Christian endeavors. "LeTourneau said, 'It pays to serve God, but if you do it because it pays, it don't pay.' If the motivation is because you want God to bless you or to make money, it won't work. You do it to honor Him."

10. *Seek and then consider the counsel of others in your business decisions.* Most companies understand the wisdom of having a board of directors. But executives need perspective from others as well, especially in the week-to-week and day-to-day operations of a business. Executives should consult fellow managers, both to float ideas and to find limits or faults. As W. N. says, "I want men who are capable of standing their ground, being strong, and following their convictions," managers who can "look me straight in the face and tell me, 'Look, you're wrong.'" Both W. N. and W. O. Meloon have had mentors to help them learn more about the business and to give them advice regarding employee relationships and business operations.

The best counsel comes from the Scriptures, W. O. believes. "The book of Proverbs has the best advice," he says. Long before business mentoring and boards of directors existed, Solomon told those seeking guidance that "in the multitude of counsellors there is safety" (Proverbs 11:14, KJV). W. O. adds, "Wise Christian counsel is a bit more important than any formula."

"THERE IS NO FORMULA"

A few years ago, a radio host asked W. O. Meloon to explain how Correct Craft survived its bankruptcy. At the end of the two-part program, the interviewer noted that three minutes remained and asked, "Mr. Meloon, in the time we have left, will you tell our audience how they can avoid getting into these difficulties?"

"There is no formula, no package that I can give that can keep people out of financial trouble," Meloon answered. "But if there *is* a formula, they will find it somewhere between Genesis 1 and the end of Revelation—in the Bible."

Likewise, W. O. cautions that the preceding ten principles are not a formula that assures business success. "There's no formula. In my experience, it has all been what God has done.

"The secular world believes formulas that you apply to your work are supposed to make you a success. Now, there can be great success in the secular world. But I don't see that success as anything like what God did with us, bringing us through bankruptcy."

W. O. believes success comes primarily from knowing God, not from following a business formula. He concludes, "I've tried both ways, and I'd rather depend on God."